LOST
New
Orleans

LOST New Orleans

MARY CABLE

Foreword by
Samuel Wilson, Jr., *F.A.I.A.*

AMERICAN LEGACY PRESS
New York

This 1984 edition is published by American Legacy Press,
distributed by Crown Publishers, Inc., by arrangement
with Houghton Mifflin Company.

Manufactured in the United States of America

Library of Congress Cataloging in Publication Data

Cable, Mary.
Lost New Orleans.

Originally published: Boston : Houghton Mifflin Co., 1980.
Bibliography: p.
Includes index.
1. Architecture—Louisiana—New Orleans. 2. New
Orleans (La.)—Buildings. 3. New Orleans (La.)—History.
I. Title
NA735.N4C32 1984   720'.9763'35   84-3005
ISBN: 0-517-448564
h g f e d c b a

Book design by David Ford

With love to
Berthe and Jimmy Amoss
of New Orleans

Acknowledgments

This book would not have been possible without the generous assistance of the Azby Fund, Edward B. Benjamin, Mr. and Mrs. Charles Keller, Jr., the E. James Kock family, and the Parkside Foundation, all of New Orleans, and of a grant from the National Endowment for the Humanities.

I am grateful to the Louisiana Landmarks Society for its sponsorship and to many of its members for their suggestions, time, and invaluable guidance in ferreting out factual errors. (If any errors remain, the fault is solely mine.) I deeply appreciated the time and trouble taken by John Geiser III, Connie G. Griffith, Betsy Swanson, Martha G. Robinson, Arthur Scully, Jr., William R. and Murray Pitts, Kirk J. Smith, and Angela Gregory; and I am especially indebted to Samuel Wilson, Jr., who spent a great deal of time reading the manuscript, offering suggestions, and writing the introduction.

Very special thanks are due to Berthe Amoss and to Thomas B. Lemann, who got me started in the first place. I also want to thank the following, all of whom went out of their way to offer help: Ann S. Gwyn and the staff of the Special Collections Division, Tulane University Library; Richard B. Allen of the William Ransom Hogan Jazz Archives, Tulane University Library; Robert R. Macdonald of the Louisiana State Museum; Collin B. Hamer, Jr., and Claudia Dumestre of the Louisiana

Division, New Orleans Public Library; Rosanne McCaffrey of the Historic New Orleans Collection; Bernard Lemann; Solis Seiferth; Marjorie Rohle; and Rosemarie Loomis and Lionel J. Bienvenu of the National Park Service. I am grateful, too, to Robert B. DeBlieux of Natchitoches, Louisiana, who sent me a splendid stack of 1911 rotogravures, and to all the others who shared old photographs.

Finally, I want to express my appreciation to Diane Maddex, of the Preservation Press, National Trust for Historic Preservation; to William Smart of the Virginia Center for the Creative Arts, where part of the book was written; and to my helpful and patient editor, Joyce Hartman, of Houghton Mifflin Company.

Contents

Foreword

When the English-born American architect, Benjamin Henry Latrobe, came to New Orleans in 1819 he was greatly impressed by the French character of the city — in its architecture and in its lifestyle. He noted regretfully the great numbers of Americans pouring into the city daily and remarked that "in a few years, therefore, this will be an American town. What is good and bad in the French manners and opinions must give way, and the American notions of right and wrong, of convenience and inconvenience will take their place." He correctly predicted that "it would be a safe wager that in 100 years not a vestige will remain of the buildings as they now stand, excepting perhaps a few public buildings and of houses built since the American acquisition of the country." Of the public buildings that he saw, only the Cabildo and the Presbytère on Jackson Square and the old Ursuline convent farther down Chartres Street have survived, along with a mere dozen or so other eighteenth-century houses.

Latrobe's predictions were largely correct, due not only to "American notions of right and wrong," but also to natural disaster: fire, hurricane, and the deleterious effect of wet soil and a humid climate. Many of the earliest French colonial buildings had been built of frame construction or *colombage,* a wood frame on sills sometimes placed directly on the ground. Such structures often rotted away within a few years. When brick became available, the French attempted to overcome this problem by building large, two-story buildings of brick such as the monumental barracks designed in 1732 by the architect-engineer Ignace François Broutin and built on the two sides of the Place d'Armes, now Jackson Square. Within twenty years these splendid and expensive structures had settled and cracked and the ends of the joints embedded in the brick walls had decayed from moisture.

Even the St. Louis Cathedral, which dominates Jackson Square and has become a recognized symbol of New Orleans, is a replacement of an earlier cathedral. The original cathedral, designed by Gilbert Guillemard and completed in 1794, replaced the first parish church of St. Louis completed in 1727 and destroyed in the great fire of 1788. The construction of the present cathedral, designed by the architect J. N. B. de Pouilly and built in 1850, was strongly opposed by the preservationists of that day. The historian Charles Gayarré thus deplored the destruction of the old Spanish landmark:

Although this monumental and venerable relic of the past was pulled down in 1850 in the mere wantonness of vandalism to make room for the upstart production of bad taste, yet the stone which covered the mortal remains of the pious founder of the destroyed temple has at least been respected.

The "pious founder" was Don Andres Almonester y Roxas, who financed the original cathedral. It was his daughter, Baroness Pontalba, who erected the handsome Pontalba buildings (1849–51), which still stand on Jackson Square, occupying the historic site of the old French barracks. The Baroness's construction of these buildings was the catalyst that resulted in the rebuilding of the cathedral, the redesign of the square and the addition of mansard roofs to the Cabildo and Presbytère.

Prior to the development of photography, lost New Orleans was preserved only in architectural drawings in French and Spanish archives, in the remarkable records in the New Orleans Notarial Archives, and in sketches made by visiting travelers and local artists. Landmarks continue to disappear, but the idea of historic preservation has become a much stronger force in the community. Historic districts have been created and additional ones are in contemplation. In spite of these positive actions, some important buildings will inevitably be destroyed in the years to come. At least, for the most part, they will be better documented in photographs, measured drawings, and original plans that are being collected in such depositories as the New Orleans Public Library, the Tulane University Library, the Louisiana State Museum and The Historic New Orleans Collection.

Books like *Lost New Orleans* enhance these collections by reaching the general public and serving as a reminder of the need to guard the heritage of the past. Such publications are a strong statement of support for the on-going preservation efforts of the Louisiana Landmarks Society and similar organizations.

Samuel Wilson, Jr. *F.A.I.A.*

New Orleans

LOST
New
Orleans

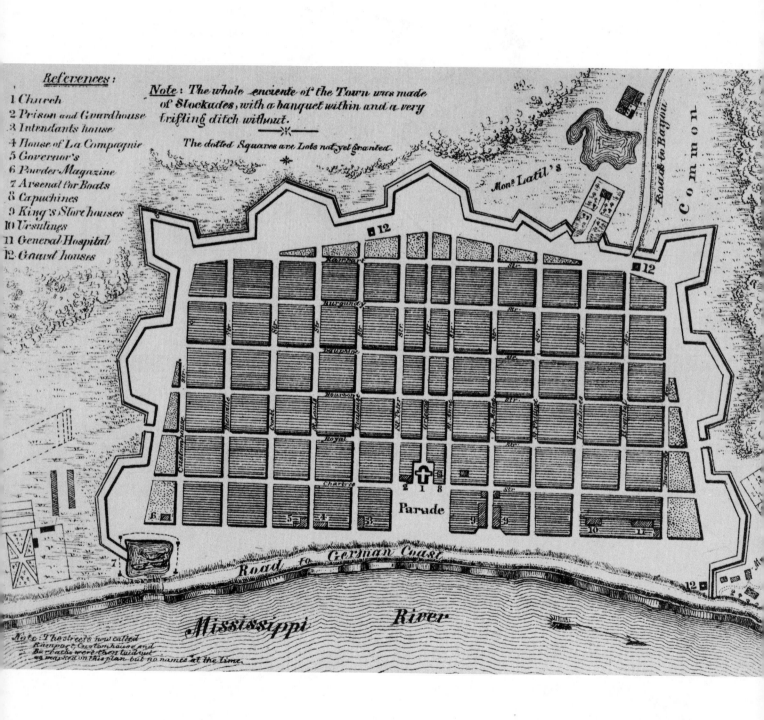

References:

1 Church
2 Prison and Guardhouse
3 Intendants house
4 House of La Compagnie
5 Governor's
6 Powder Magazine
7 Arsenal for Boats
8 Capuchines
9 King's Store houses
10 Ursulines
11 General Hospital
12 Guard houses

Note: The whole enciente of the Town was made of Stockades, with a banquet within and a very trifling ditch without.

The dotted Squares are Lots not yet granted.

Mon.ˢ Latil's

Road to Bayou

Common

12

12

Rampart

Burgundy

Dauphin

Bourbon

Royal

Charter

St. Peter

Parade

2 1 8

5   4   3   9   9   10   11

12

Road to German Coast

Mississippi River

Note: The streets now called Rampart, Customhouse and Barrack were then laid out as marked on this plan but no names at the time

1

A Village on the Mississippi

THE BEGINNINGS

All cities impose on nature, but it might be said that New Orleans doesn't just impose, it defies. Common sense had little to do with its founding, the swampy shores of the lower Mississippi being a most unwise choice as a city site. The highest point in New Orleans is fourteen feet above sea level, and in earlier times nearly all the terrain was as soft as pudding. The climate is enervating, hurricanes are an annual hazard, and until the beginning of this century the yellow-fever-bearing mosquito was a thriving local resident. Worst of all, the Mississippi is not only prone to devastating floods, but if it were not rigidly controlled by modern engineering techniques it could shift its course and leave New Orleans stranded.

Thus this unique and dynamic city of over a million* inhabitants exists despite many good reasons why it shouldn't. On land where the first settlers had difficulty in making even a log cabin stand up, there are now

* This is the population for the Greater New Orleans area. In Orleans Parish, the population as of July 1, 1977, was 561,200.

Left. Today's French Quarter still follows the neat grid of narrow streets planned in 1721. This map, made by Captain Philip Pittman, a British visitor, in 1770, shows the fortifications and the location of principal government and church buildings.

skyscrapers, expressways, and the Superdome. To support such mammoth structures, thousands of piles have to be driven through seventy feet (more or less) of muck in order to reach the Pleistocene compacted clay that underlies the entire area.

During the years of New Orleans' most spectacular growth, 1830 to 1860, builders did not have the technological knowledge to construct a Superdome, but they did succeed in putting up houses, hotels, and public buildings that were among the finest in the United States. The water table was higher then than it is now, and only a foot or two below the surface the soil was more liquid than solid. By means of pumping, laying a grillage of crossed planks that could survive under water, and using other improvised methods, architects and builders contrived to make their structures stand. But New Orleans' geographical situation — perhaps *predicament* is a better word — has always been a major factor in its history.

To understand New Orleans, one must begin with the river. The Mississippi is the city's whole raison d'être. The two have coexisted for more than two and a half centuries, sometimes with almost unbearable tension between them. For eons, the powerful waters of the river have brought silt and other debris from far to the north, building up a deltaic deposit which now extends from the vicinity of Cairo, Illinois, southward to the Gulf of Mexico. There are no rocks in or near New Orleans — scarcely a pebble, but only silt, sand, and clay mixed with decomposed swamp vegetation to produce a rich, wet soil. The delta below Baton Rouge is crisscrossed with sluggish distributaries, known as bayous, whose geographical position is unstable. Every few hundred years the great river has changed its own main course.

Before the city was founded in 1718, the inhabitants of this part of the world were seminomadic Indians. For at least ten thousand years they had been roaming here, leaving enormous middens of discarded shards and shells as evidence of their presence. If the river flooded one of their temporary villages, they simply took their few belongings and left, traveling through the alligator-infested bayous in dugout canoes.

In 1682, the French explorer Robert Cavelier, sieur de La Salle, led a small party down the Mississippi from what is now Illinois all the way to the Gulf. Near the river's mouth, La Salle put up a lead plaque, announcing that the owner of this part of the world was Louis XIV. He then made his way back up the river and returned to France from Canada. In honor of his king he named the territory he had passed through La Louisiane and the river the St. Louis. However, the Indian word *Mississippi,* said to mean "Father of Waters" or perhaps "Big River" or "Fish River" (authorities differ), was too splendid a word to be dropped from history and has managed to stay with us.

Back in Paris, La Salle had little difficulty in convincing King Louis and his ministers of the value of the new possession. Even the highly inaccurate maps at hand showed them the vast Mississippi Valley and its proximity to French possessions in Canada. They could also see the encroaching territories of rival European powers: the English ones along the Atlantic coast, the Dutch in New York, the Spanish in Florida and Mexico, and all three in the Caribbean. The fact that the Gulf end of La Louisiane was largely swamp, canebrake, alligators, and mosquitoes was of little concern to the power wielders sitting around a Paris conference table. If they stopped to picture the place at all, they probably envisioned a river mouth like that at Le Havre and other French ports, where a quiet stream flows into a deep clear harbor and the geography can be relied on to stay the same. On-the-scene reports were not very enlightening, either, because those who did the reporting were ambitious for royal grants and commissions. One letter written in 1697 to the count de Pontchartrain, minister of the Navy, described southern Louisiana as a rich, rolling country, and did not mention a word about swamps. However, even if the king and his advisors had known the unvarnished truth about the delta country, they would still have coveted it; for they were sure that if France did not move in, England or Spain would.

The king sent La Salle back to Louisiana by sea, but the new expedition failed to find the mouth of the Mississippi and landed several hundred miles west of it. While attempting to reach the Mississippi overland, La Salle was killed by his own men. It was 1699 before another expedition was dispatched, this time under a Quebecois named Pierre Le Moyne, sieur d'Iberville, who was instructed to set up a military post. Iberville built a small fort near present-day Biloxi, Mississippi, and left it garrisoned with a hundred men. When its commander died the next year, Iberville's twenty-one-year-old brother, the sieur de Bienville, succeeded him. Iberville died in 1706 in Havana of yellow fever — the disease that was to be the scourge of New Orleans. Young Bienville was to live on to stamp his name upon the early history of the city.

After a trial period, the little fort was moved to another site near present-day Mobile, and a handful of colonists struggled to make a home there. The French government sent livestock, tools, and marriageable girls. A few Canadian families arrived by way of the river. But France was now too preoccupied with a losing war against England to develop this tiny colony and, besides, after years of the excesses of Louis XIV, the royal exchequer was badly depleted. When the old king died in 1715, the country was close to bankruptcy.

Curiously enough, the future of French influence in Louisiana was ensured at this time not by a Frenchman but by a scheming Scottish gambler, John Law. Clever but reckless, Law arrived in Paris with a fortune won at the gaming tables, and made his way into French court society. The duke of Orleans, regent for the child king Louis XV, was attracted by Law's plan for making the nation solvent. This scheme called for organizing a banking company that would sell stock against the anticipated proceeds of the development of Louisiana. Law was not much of an economist, but he was a brilliant public relations man. Through beguiling publicity that extolled Louisiana's nonexistent riches, he soon had Frenchmen clamoring to invest in his Company of the West (or, as it was later called, Company of the Indies). The trouble was that few of his claims had any validity except those for agricultural possibilities — which would take many years to develop. After three years, the Mississippi "Bubble" burst, investors lost everything, and Law had to flee France for his life. Nevertheless, within that short time, one permanent step had been achieved: the settlement of New Orleans.

The French were not like the English, Spanish, or Dutch when it came to settling far shores. The French crown did not permit religious dissenters to populate the colonies as the English did; there were no gold or silver mines in Louisiana as there were in certain Spanish colonies; and the mother country was not overcrowded like Holland. So there was no reason for anyone in his right mind to want to leave *la douce France*. Yet Louisiana had to have colonists. Therefore, the king's agents emptied the jails, rounded up homeless people in the streets, and spirited away children and unguarded girls. Few of these forced immigrants appreciated their good fortune. The passage was dangerous and disagreeable and so was the arrival, which was frequently an unintentional grounding on the Gulf shore. Passengers who managed to debark safely found themselves up to their knees in a vast muddy wilderness, slapping mosquitoes and casting apprehensive glances into the impenetrable reeds around them for alligators and snakes.

In 1718, the Company of the Indies instructed the sieur de Bienville, who was still in charge of the struggling colony, to select the best city site on the lower Mississippi. All prospects were poor. Bienville chose the site of present-day New Orleans because it lay in the center of a striking crescent-shaped bend in the river and because an ancient Indian portage at the back of it led to a four-mile-long bayou, Bayou St. John, which in turn flowed into Lake Pontchartrain. The site was also a strategic point from which to monitor river traffic — if and when there was any.

Bienville landed an unwilling work crew made up of slaves, eighty convicted French smugglers, and a few trained carpenters who had been beguiled into immigrating voluntarily and set them to the excruciating job of clearing the canebrake and felling the cypresses. Even today, when excavations are being dug for new buildings, workmen sometimes find remnants of the huge cypresses cut in those first years by Bienville's laborers. Some tree trunks have measured as much as four feet in diameter.

While land was being cleared, the French engineer-in-chief Le Blond de la Tour devised a city plan, and directed the second engineer Adrien de Pauger to start laying out the streets in what eventually became a neat sixty-six-square grid. Today, the French Quarter, or Vieux Carré, has one of the oldest still-functioning street plans in North America. On the instructions of John Law, the city was named for the duke of Orleans and the streets were given royal names. In addition to Bourbon, Royal, and St. Louis, there were Burgundy (for the duke of Burgundy, father of Louis XV), Dumaine, and Toulouse, the titles of two of Louis XIV's illegitimate sons.

The first crude log houses were not very successful. They either rotted or were blown down in the hurricanes that swept the town in 1719 and 1722 or they tilted and cracked and collapsed because they had no adequate foundations. Water seeping into the streets, which often looked more like canals, made construction even more difficult. Prototypes of the typical New Orleans raised cottage — a house elevated on brick pilings six to ten or more feet off the ground — appeared very early.

For centuries, the river had been depositing soil along its banks, creating natural levees. At New Orleans, the natural levee slopes gradually toward Lake Pontchartrain, like the edge of a saucer. The colonists soon found that it was an inadequate barrier against floods and, in 1723, they began to build the first artificial levees, above and below the town as well as immediately in front of it. Thus the never-ending battle between town and river began.

A census taken in 1721 indicated a free white population of 290 men, 140 women, and 96 children. There were also 156 indentured white servants, 533 black slaves, and 50 Indian slaves. Also in Louisiana, although not in New Orleans, were several hundred Germans who had been lured by John Law's exuberant advertising into immigrating to Arkansas. After a short, disastrous time there, survivors were struggling downriver to get home again when Bienville persuaded them to settle along the river bank about fifty miles north of New Orleans. For generations thereafter they worked farms and dairies for the New Orleans markets, and some of their descendants are still ensconced on ancestral holdings in an area known as the German Coast.

By 1723 New Orleans had a hundred bark huts, a small church, some warehouses, and a house for Bienville, who was now second in command to the governor. Even he was not doing very well. He had annexed several thousand acres for himself only to have the Company of the Indies forbid a government official to own land except "as a vegetable garden." Bienville had to relinquish much of his acreage, but he retained a so-called vegetable garden of several hundred acres just beyond the edge of town, in what is now the central business district. He seems to have had a feisty disposition and he managed to alienate most of the officials sent over by the company. After a few years he was recalled to France, but in 1733, after the French government had taken over the colony from the Company of the Indies, Bienville was sent back to New Orleans for another fourteen years as governor. After that he retired to France and lived to be over eighty.

It soon became clear that Louisiana needed more ambitious and strongly motivated settlers. The Company of the Indies encouraged a few younger sons of established French families to bring modest sums of capital to the colony to start plantations. The climate was considered too debilitating for physical efforts by whites and an active slave-importing program began. The company also got together a contingent of young women, guaranteed respectable, complete with trousseaux. *Filles de la cassette,* they were called, because they carried their belongings in *cassettes,* or caskets.

The Capuchins and the Jesuits each sent a chapter and the Ursuline sisters sent a shipload of nuns. One of these young sisters, Marie Madeleine Hachard, arriving in 1727, wrote to her family to describe the new town. She said that although "there is a difference between this city and the city of Paris," New Orleans was nevertheless "very pretty, well constructed and regularly built . . . The houses are very well built of *colombage et mortier.*" This was a colonial adaptation of a medieval

Norman construction method that combined stone and timber. The colonists substituted locally made soft brick for the stone and added clay mixed with Spanish moss as insulation — an idea borrowed from the Indians. Structures made in this way were found to remain upright more successfully than if either bricks or wood were used alone.

Some of New Orleans' first buildings are shown in these drawings. At the top of the picture are barracks for workmen. Below, La Direction was a house for the directors of the West Indies Company to live and work in. It stood near the corner of Toulouse and Decatur streets. Both these buildings were designed by the city planner Le Blond de la Tour and executed under the direction of Adrien de Pauger.

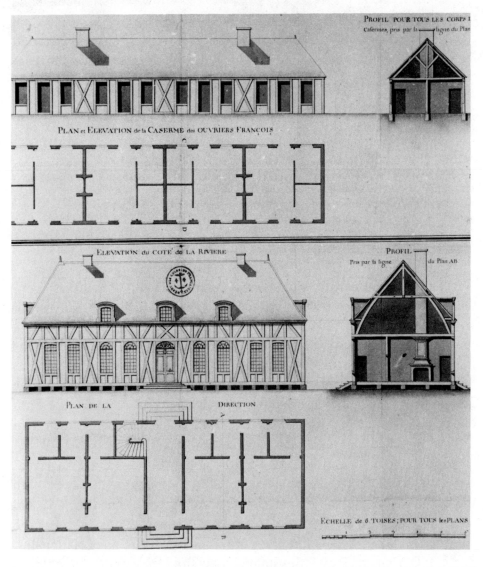

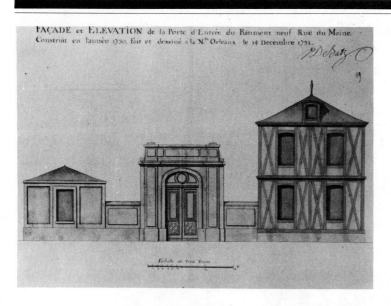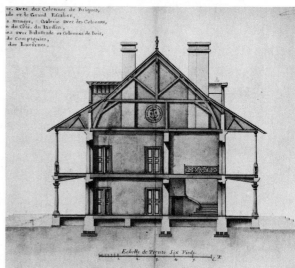

Left. A house and astronomical observatory built on the rue du Maine in 1730. The small structure at the left was the kitchen.

Middle. The signature on this sectional drawing is that of Ignace François Broutin, architect of the old Ursuline convent, which is the only eighteenth-century French building still standing in New Orleans. The house shown here, designed for the king's intendant, was never built, but its plan is the first recorded example of the French-colonial two-story gallery, which became typical of plantation houses.

''They [the houses] are white-washed, paneled, and very sunny,'' continued Marie. ''The roofs are covered with tiles which are really small pieces of wood shaped like slate. You have to see it to believe it, because these roofs look just like slate . . . Since we arrived we have been living in the best house in town. It has two stories and an attic. We have as much space as we need, with six doors leading into the rooms on the ground floor. There are big windows everywhere, however they are without panes. Instead, a thin, transparent cloth which admits as much light as glass is pulled taut inside the window frames.''

None of the buildings described by the young Ursuline have survived, nor have the more elaborate ones erected in the next few decades, with the exception of the still-extant Ursuline convent, designed in 1745 and now the oldest building in the Mississippi Valley. We know what the vanished buildings looked like from drawings in the Archives Nationales, Section Outremer, Paris. Substantial two-story buildings, including a

Shortly before the Spanish takeover, the French colonial regime of New Orleans built the substantial hip-roofed Government House.

church and a powder magazine, were constructed in the *colombage* fashion, and stuccoed with a mixture made from local lime. There was some wrought-iron ornamentation.

When the Company of the Indies gave up on New Orleans, the French Crown reluctantly took over its administration. Dog-in-the-manger politics demanded that the colony must be maintained, even though it was a liability. Bit by bit, riverfront land above and below the town was cleared for plantations, for agriculture was the only viable endeavor in the colony. A few planters became wealthy by growing indigo, tobacco, rice, corn, and a little sugar. However, sugar did not become a major crop until after 1795, when a local planter devised an effective way to crystallize it. Another commercial product, sold largely to the West Indies, was a candle made from the wax of myrtle trees.

The French government showed concern for its struggling colonists, even giving them what nowadays is known as emergency relief. An English traveler wrote, "The planter is considered as a Frenchman venturing his life, enduring a species of banishment, and undergoing great hardships for the benefit of his country; for which reason he has great indulgences shewn. Whenever by hurricanes, earthquakes, or bad seasons, the planters suffer, a stop is put to the rigor of exacting creditors. The few taxes which are levied are remitted, and even advances are made to repair their losses and set them forward."

The planters evolved a house that was ideally suited to their way of life and to the climate. It had a hip roof that came down like an umbrella over wide porches called galleries (from the French *galerie,* "long room"). In the earliest examples, these galleries surrounded the interior on all sides, protecting it from sun and rain. The windows were as wide and tall as the doors and had louvered shutters (*jalousies*). Ceilings were high. If the house had a second story it was reached by a staircase on one of the galleries, because, in accordance with traditional French house design, there was no hallway. There were usually two large rooms at the front, opening into three smaller ones at the rear. To avoid unnecessary heat in the house, the kitchen was a separate outbuilding. A central chimney provided warmth for the short but chilly winter. The house, raised well off the ground by brick piers, was built of local cypress, a wood that

This plantation house, built in the late seventeenth or early eighteenth century, belonged to a brother of Bernard de Marigny, the founder of Faubourg Marigny and at one time one of the wealthiest men on this continent. The drawing, made in 1835, is part of a remarkable collection, unparalleled in any other city. Throughout the nineteenth century, whenever a house came up for public auction, the sheriff's office had a drawing made of it, which was later filed away in the Notarial Archives. During the 1930s, the WPA rescued these drawings from neglect, catalogued them, and preserved them.

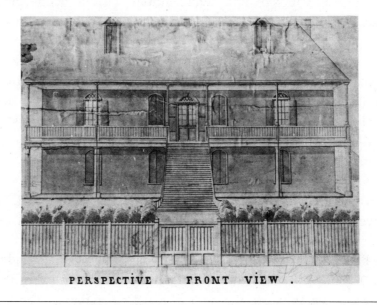

PERSPECTIVE FRONT VIEW .

proved splendidly resistant to water, insects, and fungus. Although very few eighteenth-century plantation houses remain in the New Orleans area, the influence of some of these early architectural ideas is still evident.

Because river frontage was essential to the commercial operation of a plantation, the land on the river was granted or sold in long, narrow strips, the narrow side bordering the water. The planter's house stood near the front of the property, with the slave quarters behind it. Behind the quarters were the fields and behind those the uncleared cypress swamp, where in winter the slaves were put to work chopping trees and operating sawmills. Each planter was responsible for keeping his part of the levee in good repair. A crevasse, or crack, in the levee was a disaster, not only for those in the immediate vicinity but for neighbors up and down the river and for the town itself. The usual cause of a crevasse was the force of the current against a cut bank when the river was high. Carelessness or inefficiency might also be a factor, and there were instances of deliberate opening of a levee as an act of hostility against a landowner. New Orleans was thus at the mercy of the outlying planters and remained so for well over a century. In 1849, for example, a crevasse upriver put almost the entire city under water for three weeks. Only the installation of modern pumps and sewers, early in this century, finally spared New Orleans the disasters that come from a break in the levee.

·

Jean-Bernard Bossu, a Frenchman who visited the colony in the early 1750s, wrote that the ruling class lived a life of no little luxury, importing French furnishings for their houses and regaling themselves with French wines and delicacies. One might walk into a simple plantation house and find it furnished with elegant carved chairs and tables, gilded pier glasses, and Turkish carpets. The table might be set with Sèvres and the guests dressed in French velvets and laces. Such amenities apparently mattered more to the planters than education. There were no good schools in the colony. Boys were sometimes sent to France for an education, but, Bossu noted, "as for the fair sex, whose only duty is to please, they are already born with that advantage here and do not have to go to Europe to acquire it artificially." Being French, the people cherished the graces of life — wit, charm, and manners; and social life for the upper classes and for skilled laborers (for skills were scarce and commanded respect) had its agreeable aspects. But on the whole, the provincial, isolated town on the Mississippi River was still a hardship post.

In 1763, at the end of the war that was called the Seven Years War in Europe and the French and Indian War in North America, a political event took place that could never happen today. Even in that time of autocracies it seemed slightly highhanded. The Bourbon king of France, Louis XV, sat down with his first cousin, the Bourbon Charles III of Spain, and arranged by secret treaty to deed the colony of Louisiana to Spain. France was glad to be rid of a losing investment, while Spain believed it wise to acquire this vast piece of territory contiguous to its Mexican and Floridian holdings to make sure that it did not fall into the hands of England. The people of New Orleans were not only unconsulted but were not even told about the treaty until two years later.

When the colonists heard of their change of nationality they could scarcely believe it. Some of the leading citizens got together and went to Paris to beg His Majesty to reconsider. According to one often-told story, Bienville, then a very old man, went with them. They were received by the foreign minister, the duke of Choiseul, who had urged the king to cede Louisiana. Despite Bienville's tearful pleading, the meeting was useless. A Spanish governor arrived in 1766. The fact that he brought with him only ninety soldiers made some of the colonists decide on open rebellion and they took the desperate step of driving the governor and the Spanish soldiers out. However, except for one or two among them who had been in Europe and had heard of Republicanism, the rebels cherished no notion of governing themselves. They merely wished to put their heads back under the old yoke rather than under the new.

Charles III of Spain was no despot, but he could not countenance revolution. He sent one of his most capable generals, the Irish-born Alejandro O'Reilly, to take the matter in hand. With O'Reilly went not ninety soldiers but 2600. Debarking just below the town, they marched into it to the sound of music and drums, cannon salvos, and small arms fire. O'Reilly promptly imprisoned the ringleaders of the rebellion and had them tried and punished, some by death, others by prison terms that were commuted later. So ended the effort of the New Orleanians to assert themselves openly. In a more subtle way, however, they asserted themselves very well. The city was still French in language and custom and, although the Spanish ruled it for more than thirty-five years, they succeeded in leaving a lasting mark only on the architecture.

As the old French buildings of New Orleans deteriorated, new ones were built in the Spanish manner. Doors and windows were usually arched and roofs were covered in Spanish tile. In the town, larger L-shaped

Left. A typical tile-roofed Spanish cottage, on Royal Street, built as a school during the Spanish regime and used as a courthouse during the early years of the Americans. It was razed in 1888. Here, in 1815, Andrew Jackson was fined $1000 for contempt of court by a judge he had antagonized. The money was later repaid to Jackson by order of Congress.

Middle and right. Very little of colonial New Orleans survived into the twentieth century. Here is an eighteenth-century shop in the 500 block of Chartres Street (demolished in 1929), and an old Spanish tiled cottage, long since gone.

houses were built, with the short side facing the street and a courtyard in the angle. Some houses had flat roofs so that families could have roof gardens where children could play and old people take the air without going into the wet and dirty streets. The Spanish used wrought iron lavishly: for balconies, for decorative lanterns, latches, doorhandles, and keyholes. Some of it was probably brought from southern Spain or from Mexico and some was made locally by slaves and free persons of color (that is, freed blacks, or persons of mixed African and Caucasian blood who had been born free or who had been given their freedom).

The Spanish — and sometimes the French — were fond of painting stucco houses in pastel colors such as pale blue, apricot, yellow, and light green. The Spanish urban house was often built with an entresol — a service floor between the first and second stories. This floor was lit by small windows and was used for storage.

John Smyth, an Englishman who sojourned in New Orleans in 1784, termed the houses "pretty good, and they may amount in number to three or four hundred." On the whole, he found New Orleans "rather a disagreeable place," but he added that if the British took it over it would improve. Captain Philip Pittman of His Majesty's Army, an Englishman who was in New Orleans a decade earlier, thought even less of the place. The cathedral, he wrote, was falling down and services had to be held in a storehouse. The governor had no suitable residence and had to rent a house owned by a former agent of the Company of the Indies. To the old French palisade around the town the Spanish had added a moat — "a trifling ditch," Pittman wrote. Neither palisade nor moat were strong enough to repel an armed force, but perhaps they provided some security against a slave uprising. A garrison of 400 soldiers prevented the "slaves of the town and country from having any communication in the night." After curfew, the gates were locked, for the fear of a slave insurrection was always present among the whites.

Spanish rule was more repressive than French as far as foreign contacts were concerned. The colony was forbidden to trade with any country other than Spain. But officials were corruptible and there were many infringements of the law. English trading ships took to sailing up from the Gulf and anchoring opposite the town. There they carried on a lively illicit trade, selling at wildly elevated prices fancy foods and dry goods that were otherwise unobtainable in New Orleans. Like the French, the Spanish colonists were fond of luxuries. When Spain took the American side in our Revolution, a few American traders were able to get special trading privileges in New Orleans. Although the Spanish, like the French before them, prohibited Protestants and Jews from living in the colony, the law was not strictly enforced.

In March 1788, on Good Friday, a fire started due to candles left unattended on a private altar. The usual fire alarm was the ringing of church bells, but, so the story goes, the priests were shocked at the idea of ringing bells on Good Friday and by the time they were persuaded to do so, the fire was out of hand and in a few hours it wiped out nearly 900 of the town's 1100 buildings. Only six years later, another fire, which by some accounts was caused by children playing with fire near a hay store on a windy day, again decimated most of New Orleans. There were no fire-fighting equipment and firemen, volunteer or paid. The fires were fought by householders and soldiers, carrying buckets of water.

There was now very little left of the French colonial town, except the

Ursuline convent. During the 1790s, the present Cabildo and Presbytère were built and a wealthy citizen named Don Andres Almonester y Roxas financed St. Louis Cathedral. In the same decade, Governor Carondelet, more enterprising than many Spanish governors, oversaw the construction of a canal, which enabled small craft to enter the city via Bayou St. John from Lake Pontchartrain.

But, by and large, Spanish New Orleans was not an up-and-coming place. C. C. Robin, a French traveler who visited the city in 1802, was distressed by the lack of planning among the colonists. He wrote:

The inhabitants are preoccupied with the present and have no regard for the future. [They] seem to see in trees only obstacles to their labors. They do not see them as attractive to the eyes, nor do they see the necessity of these majestic plants for shade and for purifying the air . . . I have seen respected citizens, in choosing a cypress for some purpose, make a game of cutting down a large number which they simply left dying.

I find this taste for destroying native production stems from the maxim that we teach to children that the earth is given to man to enjoy. From this teaching, the child concludes that he is at liberty to change, upset, or destroy anything he pleases, according to his whim. Instead of this erroneous notion he should be taught that man is the foremost of creatures only because he is the foremost conservationist; that the most meritorious of activities is the preservation of his environments; that he should enjoy everything; but misuse nothing; and that even in the least of creatures he should recognize the work of the creator. Then he would submit to authority in the wilderness as in human society.

The wanton destruction of natural resources was not a trait that belonged exclusively to the people of New Orleans. It was a way of life all over North America and, as Americans began to come into contact with the little delta city, they brought their own extravagant and reckless ideas with them, applying them also to buildings, which like trees were regarded as totally expendable.

By the end of the century a good many Americans were turning up in New Orleans. Rough frontiersmen brought keelboats down the Mississippi with cargoes of pickled pork, cornmeal, and whiskey. The Spanish and French traded with these people and bought broken-up keelboats to use for sidewalks, wharves, and houses, but they kept their distance socially, considering all Americans to be unspeakably lacking in refinement. The joy experienced by the French population when, in 1802, it became known that Spain was voluntarily handing over the colony to the Napoleonic regime in France turned into major shock only a few months later when the French emperor sold Louisiana to the Americans. The sorrow and rage among the people of New Orleans was even greater than it had been

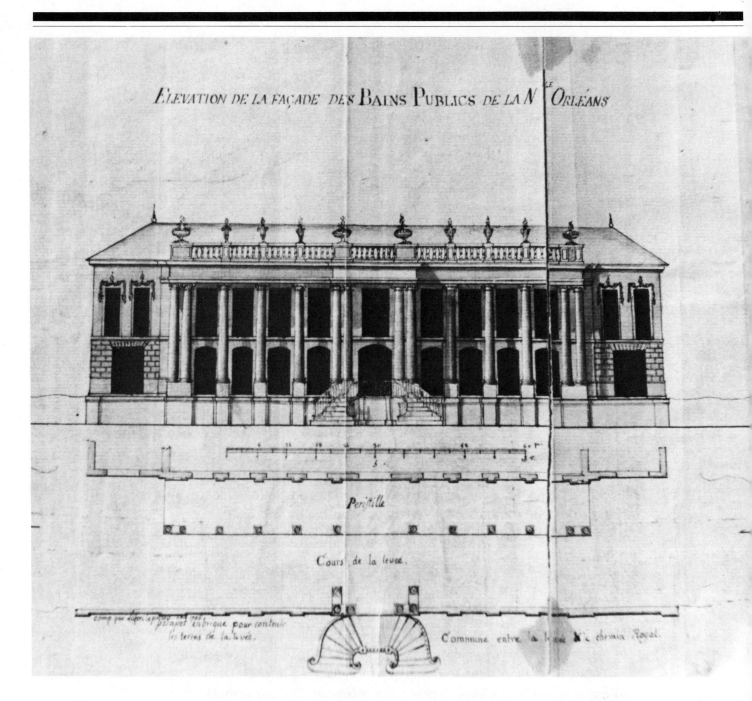

When Bartholemy Lafon made this ambitious design for a public bath in 1796, he had just arrived in the colony, an unknown engineer and architect. The bath was never built, but Lafon went on to leave his stamp on New Orleans by executing Bernard de Marigny's plans for Faubourg Marigny and by his own remarkable city planning.

in the 1760s. Back then, the French had not wanted Spanish rule, but at least the Spanish were Catholic and monarchists and shared a Latin language with the French. Despite the shortcomings of Spanish rule, the city had grown and prospered. In 1760, the white population had been 3200 and now it was 8000, swelled by settlers from the Canary Islands and Malaga and by French refugees from the slave uprisings in Santo Domingo. Now the local people of both nationalities were united in an anguished outcry against rule by Protestants, Republicans, and English-speaking nobodies and they predicted nothing but total ruin for New Orleans.

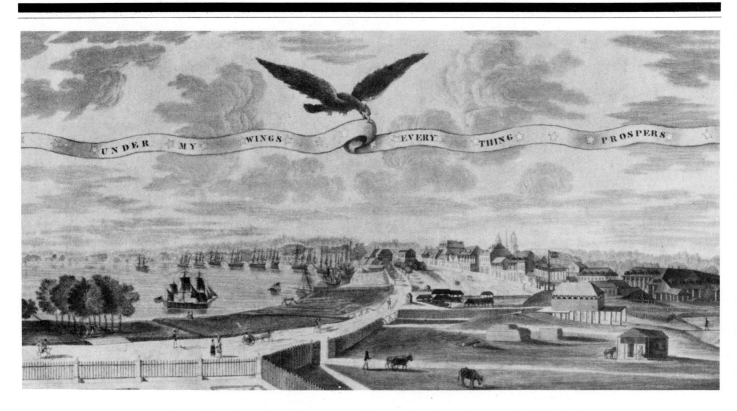

A view of American New Orleans soon after the Louisiana Purchase in 1803. Faubourg Marigny had not yet been developed, and the levee was still a pleasant place to walk.

2

"Under My Wings Everything Prospers"

TRANSPORTATION AND COMMERCE

John Pintard, a New York merchant, visited Spanish New Orleans in 1801, as it waited, sleepy and unknowing, for its extraordinary destiny. Pintard wrote long letters home, describing what appeared to him to be a backward little town. "Some few houses may be called handsome," he said, but added that their furnishings were plain. "Indeed, I do not remark much display of taste — either within or without doors — All luxury confined to what is put on the table to be eaten, and here profusion abounds." He noted that real estate prices were very high, and "There is no such thing as cleaning the streets that I have seen, further than dragging the mud from the gutters into the middle of the street — when the powerful influence of the sun soon exhales the stench and dries up the filth . . . The few carriages that roll the Streets were introduced at least before the French ceded this country to Spain in 1762 — with the exception of some few second hand carriages which have been transported here for being out of fashion ten years ago in the United States. The horses however are a dead match for the sad vehicles they drag."

Pintard was gracious enough to admire the cathedral and the Cabildo, and noted a convent of nuns, two orders of friars, a barracks, an arsenal, and some fortifications ("I believe these works very inadequate — But I am no engineer.") He objected to the cumbersome Spanish requirement that all incoming vessels unload their goods for examination at the custom house — "a very tedious and disagreeable mode of business as ever was contrived." The meat market was "the most filthy I have ever seen — whether it be ever hoed out or not I cannot say." On the other hand, fish and shellfish were abundant and excellent and so were vegetables, eggs, poultry, and game birds. As for bread, "it equals any in the world — It was a high relish to my appetite after going into a bakery & seeing a number of Negroes without shirts — & almost naked sweating over the kneading troughs — I was rightly served — no person who has any squeamishness ought ever to thrust his nose into French Cuzine." The only forms of entertainment seem to have been gambling, which was very popular, and walking on the levee, "which is eternally thronged with all sorts & conditions of people . . . It is about 8 feet wide, the slope towards the river presents all the shipping of the harbour with their usual concomitants of noisey [sic] drunken labourers and sailors — over and above what is incident to other ports are the River Boats of all dimensions — with their crews at evening cooking their suppers at a multitude of Fires kindled all along shore."

Pintard's lukewarm sentiments toward New Orleans probably would have been shared by most middle-class Americans of his time. Nevertheless, after the Louisiana Purchase, hundreds of just such people migrated there in the hope of making their fortunes. For, as Thomas Jefferson had said of New Orleans nearly twenty years earlier, "no such position for the accumulation and perpetuity of wealth and power ever existed."

Wealth and power were important everywhere in the young United States, but for the Americans who went to New Orleans they were often an obsession. Some regarded their stay in New Orleans as temporary and dreamed of returning whence they had come, rich and leisured. Others fell in love with the place and sent for their families, or married local girls, as soon as they could afford it. It was said that an intelligent, hardworking young man, starting at the bottom, could become a partner in a business, or even own it, within ten or twelve years; and this actually happened often enough for the news of it to attract other aspirants.

The Mississippi River, of course, was the compelling reason for the city's potential, as it was the reason for its existence in the first place. Commerce began and ended on the levees, for here cargoes from abroad arrived for sale or transshipment, and cargoes from upriver were loaded into ocean-going vessels. Warehouses were therefore the first large new buildings to be needed in American New Orleans.

During the Spanish regime, the levee had been a favorite promenade for citizens of the town. For twenty or more years into the nineteenth century it continued to be a place for people until little by little it was overtaken by the demands of commerce. Welcome Arnold Greene, an 1823 visitor from Rhode Island, reported that a walk down the levee was "very beautiful, the fronts of their houses being literally blooming gardens." A walk *up* the levee, however, took one among warehouses and wagons and within sniffing distance of the slaughterhouses upriver.

New Orleans' immediate hinterland, the bayou country, was of little

In the early days of American New Orleans, the riverfront was lined with commercial buildings like this one of Hoover & Pearce. The Hoover family, or the Pearces, or both, probably lived on the upper floors.

commercial importance to the city, except as a source of fresh food. The real hinterland was hundreds of miles upriver: such cities as St. Louis, Cincinnati, Cairo, and Duluth as well as newer ones on the Red, the Missouri, and other tributaries of the Mississippi. As if New Orleans' geographical catbird seat was not enough, two inventions — the cotton gin and the steamboat — came along at just the right moment.

By 1830 cotton was the chief crop of southern planters and they sent it to market in New Orleans via steamboat. Enormous cotton presses were built, fronting on the river. "No architectural effect was aimed at in the facade, which is, however, neat and plain," said *Norman's Guide to New Orleans* (1845), speaking of the Levee Steam Cotton Press, which cost half a million dollars to build in 1832. The even larger Orleans Cotton Press burned to the ground in 1844 in one of New Orleans' many spectacular fires; and there were others. Cotton presses were vital to the port. They compressed the bales of cotton sent in from plantations so that three times as many could be stowed into holds. Each bale had already been compressed by plantation wooden presses and weighed about 450 pounds, but the steam press reduced them further. The Orleans Cotton Press could process 300,000 bales a year.

The growing of cotton (or of sugar, the other major southern crop) required the labor of thousands of slaves. In 1806 Congress outlawed the importation of slaves into the United States, but in the boundless swamps of the lower delta this was a difficult law to enforce. Between New Orleans and the Gulf was a pirate stronghold called Barataria and there shiploads of "prime African Negroes" were often inexplicably available. Planters could find a discreet way of replenishing their supply of field hands from Barataria. For at least the first quarter of the nineteenth century, known pirates mingled openly with businessmen in the New Orleans exchanges. They seem to have been tolerated by the general public and sometimes even admired. In his book *Life on the Mississippi,* Mark Twain slyly tells the story of one pirate who "retired" to New Orleans and became an alderman:

He was a pirate with a tremendous and sanguinary history; and as long as he preserved unspotted, in retirement, the dignity of his name and the grandeur of his ancient calling, homage and reverence were his from high and low; but when at last he descended into politics and became a paltry alderman, the public "shook" him, and turned aside and wept. When he died they set up a monument over him; and little by little he has come into respect again; but it is respect for the pirate, not the alderman. To-day the loyal and generous remember only what he was, and charitably forget what he became.

Native-born slaves were more desirable than "fresh" Africans, who were not easy to train and manage. Virginia slaves, regarded as well trained and intelligent, brought the highest prices. New Orleans became the biggest slave market in the south, and numerous yards, jails, and camps (all names for the compounds where slaves were assembled before being sold) were to be found in the neighborhood of Camp Street. Slaves

By the 1850s, it was customary for slaves being auctioned to be neatly attired in suits, shirts, ties, and high hats — like those seen here through the open door at 156 Common Street. There were at least twenty-five slave yards or "jails" in the downtown area, where slaves were held for sale. The law forbade dealers to display this type of merchandise on the sidewalk, lest it prove an annoyance to ladies passing by. The Danish writer Frederika Bremer, who visited one of these markets in the 1850s, described "a cold, dirty hall," many customers, and black men and women, "silent and serious," standing against the walls. "I saw nothing especially repulsive in these places," wrote Miss Bremer, "excepting the whole thing."

were sold in buildings constructed for that purpose, as well as in auction rooms in the city's most elegant hotels.

Before the advent of the Mississippi steamboat in 1812, anyone who wished to transport merchandise (human or otherwise) down the river had to do it by flatboat or keelboat. A flatboat could only go with the current; a keelboat could, with difficulty, be navigated upstream. Navigating a loaded keelboat took two men, who might be the owners of it or who might work for some small entrepreneur. In 1827, young Abraham Lincoln and a friend made two keelboat journeys to New Orleans from a point on the Ohio near Rockport, Illinois. They were paid $8 a month by the keelboat owner, and the round trip took three months. In New Orleans they sold the keelboat for its timbers, which were much in demand for building and for making sidewalks, and returned to Illinois by steamboat.

During the first trip, Lincoln acquired a lifelong scar over his right eye, fighting with a band of thieves who attacked them while they were tied up overnight. What Lincoln thought of "Orlins," the first big city he ever saw, is not recorded, nor whether he tried any of its wicked pastimes as most keelboatmen did. Some say that he saw a slave auction and that he made up his mind then to free the slaves. What New Orleans thought of Lincoln certainly was not much, for keelboatmen were generally regarded as a very low form of life. Kaintucks they were called, and they helped give the New Orleans riverfront its reputation for rowdiness and violence.

After steam came to the river, keelboat and flatboat traffic was no longer vital, but independent traders still continued to operate, bringing anything that would float, but mostly corn and pork products and whiskey. In 1846, for example, 2670 of these vessels made port. The same year, New Orleans also received 518 schooners, 377 barks, 447 brigs, and 2763 steamboats. The total number of steamboats on the river that year was 550, which meant that most of them called at New Orleans four or five times.

Under the escort of a pilot ocean-going ships could ply between the Gulf and New Orleans, provided they were able to clear the bar at Belize — which sometimes had to be dredged while ships waited in the Gulf for weeks and even months. The journey upriver took eight or nine days by oar or sail and from twelve to twenty-four hours by steam. As the city was approached, desolate swamps and woods on both banks gave way to handsome plantations. Passengers stood on deck, looking impatiently for the first sign of New Orleans. In Spanish days, this had been the twin spires of the St. Louis Cathedral. The Americans built an assortment of new church spires, some reaching higher. And from 1835 to 1851 when it burned, one of the highest points was the great white dome of the first St. Charles Hotel.

"The first view of the town from the river is very striking," wrote Mrs. Houstoun, an Englishwoman, arriving in her husband's yacht in 1842. "I think I never saw, in any other, so long and continuous a line of large, and even grand-looking buildings. The innumerable lights which gleamed from the houses and public buildings and which were reflected in the river were to us, so long unused to the cheerful aspect of a large and bustling city, a most welcome sight."

This smoky scene on the levee in 1883 showed the return of prosperity to post-Reconstruction New Orleans.

The levee was divided into stations for the various types of craft. Flatboats anchored upstream, in the vicinity of what is now the Garden District. In the main part of the city, steamboats were four deep. The downstream position was reserved for sailing ships, also four deep. The outer vessels were unloaded by stevedores who walked back and forth across the decks of those nearer shore. All in all, the riverfront was a

This photograph taken in 1895 shows the Old Basin at the head of the Carondelet Canal a hundred years after it was constructed. Named for Louis Hector, baron de Carondelet, the enterprising Spanish governor who tried to joggle New Orleans out of its colonial lethargy, the canal enabled seagoing vessels to enter the city from Lake Pontchartrain by way of Bayou St. John. Well into this century it was still in use.

fascinating and astonishing sight. In 1837, another English visitor wrote, ". . . the whole margin of the river as you look down upon it from the levee, or from the roof of Bishop's Hotel on a sunny morning after a night of storm, when the sails of the whole are exposed to the air, and their signals or national flags abroad, is one of the most singularly beautiful you can conceive."

When the ships were loaded and ready to sail they stood out in the stream, waiting for a pilot that towed two or three vessels at a time, "like a covey of partridges in the talons of an eagle," Mrs. Houstoun wrote.

Another way of arriving by water was via Lake Pontchartrain. This route was used by vessels from Mobile and other points on the Gulf Coast, and was preferred by captains of small sailing craft in order to avoid the swift current of the river. The Carondelet Canal, which Governor Carondelet had caused to be dug in the 1790s, was connected to Bayou St. John and was full of silt and needed constant dredging. In 1832 a company was organized to build a wider and deeper canal, six and a half miles long, from Rampart Street, at the back of the American part of the city, to the lake. The digging took six years and many lives, the laborers dying not only of sunstroke and malaria but also in epidemics of cholera and yellow fever. When the canal was completed in 1835, small vessels could enter the city as far as the New Basin.

Until 1825, New Orleans enjoyed a monopoly of trade between the Northeast and the Middle West. That year the Erie Canal was completed and suddenly New Orleans merchants and brokers who had been happily amassing fortunes on commissions realized that this unprecedented Yankee enterprise, which people had been scoffing at, was going to cause trouble. Many shippers would now find it cheaper and faster to send goods by the canal rather than by river and sea. It was only a small cloud in New Orleans' bright sky, but it did break the monopoly and from then on the cloud grew larger. Other canals were built in the North and then, only a few years later, came the first railroads. Any fool could see that if there were going to be railroads in the North, the South must have them, too.

Railroad fever broke out in the New Orleans business community and by 1840 there were twenty-three railroad companies in Louisiana — at least on paper. The state should have coordinated the railroads' efforts and winnowed some of them out, but failed to do so. The result was that useless miles of track were constructed and routes that were clearly hopeless were surveyed. One group of entrepreneurs dreamed of a railroad from New Orleans to the Gulf, through many miles of soggy swamp and across open bays forty feet deep. This company, the Mexican Gulf Line, laid nineteen miles of track, taking it as far as the neighboring parish of St. Bernard, and went bankrupt. Bankruptcy was the fate of nearly all the railroad companies and this contributed in a major way to the financial panic of 1837 when fourteen out of the sixteen banks in New Orleans closed their doors.

Nevertheless, railroad fever brought two successful railroad lines to the city. The first was the Pontchartrain, the third oldest in the United States. It ran from the levee, at the foot of Elysian Fields, to the lake, a distance of 5.18 miles. It carried passengers to and from ships that arrived at New Orleans by way of the lake and it also brought excursionists who came from the city for the day, or, later, after a hotel was built, for a summer holiday. Fortunes were made in lakeside lots and acreages. In the same fashion, the New Orleans & Carrollton Railroad helped to develop the upriver suburbs and Carrollton itself. The owners had to agree not to

Beginning in 1835, pleasure-seekers could take the New Orleans & Carrollton Railroad to the water. At the old Carrollton Hotel (background) they might have had a meal or perhaps spent a summer holiday.

allow their trains to travel more than four miles an hour and they promised that if people declared the whole thing a nuisance they would remove it. The New Orleans & Carrollton, which was begun in 1833, was less difficult to build than the Pontchartrain (since its route did not lie through swamps), but after it was finished there was a year's wait for a locomotive to arrive from England. The maiden journey from Canal Street to Carrollton took place on September 26, 1835. The same ground is still being traveled, twenty-four hours a day, by some of the last trolleys left in the United States, the St. Charles Avenue line. (The streetcar named Desire turned into a bus named Desire some time ago.)

Oakey Hall, the author of *The Manhattaner in New Orleans* (1851), said that the Pontchartrain railroad station was a long building "consecrated to emptiness," and resembled the horse shed of a New England meeting house. The age of palatial railroad stations came in the late

---

The only railroad station ever designed by Louis Sullivan was this one, for the Illinois Central Railroad, in 1892. Sullivan said that the long hip roof of the building was inspired by Creole plantation houses he had seen from train windows in the deep South. In the 1950s, the station was replaced by the Union Passenger Terminal.

Above. Daniel Burnham, architect for Washington's Union Station, also designed this monumental station at Canal and Basin streets. Completed in 1908, it was intended as a central terminal for several lines, but was actually used only by the Southern Railroad.

Below. Another of New Orleans' numerous railroad stations, all now demolished, was the Trans Mississippi Terminal at Annunciation and Terpsichore streets.

nineteenth and early twentieth century. At that time New Orleans acquired two new stations designed by the nation's most prominent architects: the Illinois Central Station, designed in 1892 by Louis Sullivan (Frank Lloyd Wright, then a young man in Sullivan's office, worked on the drawings); and a terminal at Canal and Basin streets, designed by Daniel Burnham, and completed in 1908. The latter was intended for the joint use of several railroads, but was actually used only by the Southern Railroad. Both of these handsome buildings have been demolished.

·

Memoirs and travelers' reports of New Orleans never fail to mention the markets: the immense variety of their produce, their colorfulness, and the Tower of Babel sound of overheard talk. The prevailing languages were French, Creole* patois, English, and Spanish, but one also heard German, Gaelic, Choctaw, Greek, and Maltese; and as time went by, a large admixture of Italian. In earlier days there were newly imported slaves who knew only their tribal languages, and, always, there were sailors — and pirates — conversing in languages from every port in the world.

Most of the Indians in or near New Orleans were Choctaws — the indigenous Indians had become extinct before 1800. The Choctaws, miserably poor and living in the nearby swamps, would come to the market to sell baskets and sassafras root, with which Creole cooks made filé powder for gumbo. Early descriptions of these Indians describe them as honest and quiet, but later they seem to have fallen victim to alcoholism. "Choctaws reeling drunk in Father Adam's costume," one observer noted, "a well worn, diaphanous blanket being substituted for the historical fig leaf."

At the Place d'Armes (the present Jackson Square), wooden steps led from the top of the levee, and here market boats moored each day, bringing all sorts of fish and shellfish, game, vegetables, and fruit. Benjamin Latrobe, the nationally famous architect who came to live in New Orleans in 1819, noticed market boats flying Napoleonic pennants. During Napoleon's imprisonment on St. Helena, Bonapartists hatched a plot to

---

* Webster's *New International Dictionary*, second edition, quotes George Washington Cable's definition of the word *Creole*: "The title [Creole] did not first belong to the descendants of Spanish, but of French, settlers. But such a meaning implied a certain excellence of origin, and so came early to include any native of French or Spanish descent by either parent, whose nonalliance with the slave race entitled him to social rank. Later, the term was adopted by, not conceded to, the natives of mixed blood, and is still so used among themselves." As an adjective, the meaning is defined as follows: "Of, pertaining to, or characteristic of, a Creole or Creoles . . . manufactured or produced by Creoles; loosely, peculiar to Louisiana; as, Creole shoes, eggs, wagons, baskets, etc."

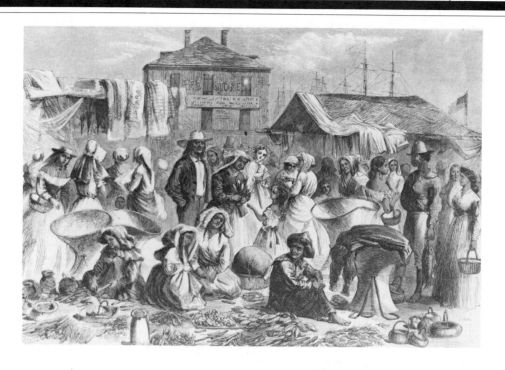

Left. The open-air markets of New Orleans were once among its special pleasures. Today a few remain; among them is the famous French Market, now considerably tidied up and sanitized. The top picture shows the exotic assortment of customers and vendors that were once seen there. Near the French Market was the Red Store (below), one of the oldest buildings on the waterfront. It was torn down in the 1930s, but rebuilt in the 1970s on a nearby site.

Above. One of many markets in various parts of the city was the Prytania Street Market, between Lyons and Upperline streets. The roof and turrets seen here in the background are those of an old school, which is still standing.

rescue him and bring him to New Orleans, using the services of local pirates.

At one corner of Jackson Square (now known as the French Market) was the first, largest, and most important market, but there were many others, such as St. Mary's Market, on Tchoupitoulas Street; the Prytania Street market; the Vegetable Market (which had Roman Doric columns) at Old Levee Street and the river; and the Poydras Street Market (with two giant horns of plenty in bas relief over the main entrance). All were long, roofed, open-air structures, and all except the French Market have now disappeared.

There was no end to the delightful edibles for sale: local specialties, such as *calas tout chauds* (fried cakes), pralines, poor boy sandwiches (some say the name derived from the French *pourboire*, ''a tip''), *estomac mulâtre* (gingerbread), and a kind of hot oyster sandwich that was a favorite restorative for carousers at the end of a night on the town. Then, there were all the seasonings used in Creole cooking: onions, garlic, bay leaf, hot peppers, thyme, basil, cloves, nutmeg, allspice, and filé powder.

New Orleanians ate a great deal of meat, although good quality was hard to find. One might have better luck with raccoon, bear, rabbit, or possum brought in by hunters than with the tough beef that had arrived from Texas on the hoof. John James Audubon, who lived in New Orleans in 1820, noted that he saw many kinds of wild birds for sale at the market. Besides the usual game birds, there was a large variety of songbirds, whose tiny bodies made only morsels. In his journal, Audubon observed, ''Much surprised and diverted was I in finding a Barred Owl, cleaned and exposed, for sale at twenty-five cents.'' Audubon, it may be noted, was not much of a conservationist. He loved painting birds, but he also loved shooting them and seems to have suffered no pang in recording that during the migration season as many as 144,000 golden plovers were shot in a day.

Because the markets were considered too rough for ladies, it was a Creole tradition for gentlemen to do the marketing for their households. American men, much too busy making money, sent their slaves. Eliza Ripley, who was brought up on Canal Street in the 1840s, all her life remembered the delights of marketing with one of her father's most trusted servants, always stopping to spend a picayune for some spicy or sugary treat. Citizens who could not get to the market were able to buy a wide variety of food from peddlers who set up temporary stalls or circulated through the streets, hawking their wares in two languages. Because the

streets were so dirty and the markets so rough, many housewives preferred to buy all they could from their own doorsteps. The milkman made
regular rounds with a horse and wagon, ringing a bell to announce his
approach and dispensing milk from large tin cans in a hopelessly unsani-
tary fashion. Most vendors pushed two-wheeled handcarts, and alternated
their cries with the blowing of a tin trumpet or the ringing of a triangle.
Besides milk and produce, they specialized in all sorts of prepared food:
bons petits calas, tout chauds, or *confitures cocos,* or *fromage Creole* as
well as fried oysters, coconut cakes, and ice cream. There were also
caterers, who could deliver complete hot meals, individually packed in a
three-compartmented metal container. Other street criers advised the

The city streets were once the province of countless roving vendors — like this old fruit
seller.

public of various services: scissors grinding, chimney sweeping, tin smithery, and the like. And there were peddlers who were one-man dry-goods stores, selling all sorts of cheap fabrics, buttons, and ribbons.

But if one wanted fine, imported goods, one went to the shops. Until the late 1840s, elegant shopping centered along Royal Street and Chartres Street (pronounced, under the American influence, *Charters*). Here was the equivalent of Bond Street or Fifth Avenue. On a fine day, these streets were thronged with pretty, well-dressed women going in and out of the shops, and the sight of them drove one ante-bellum visitor, Edward Mackie, to journalistic excesses such as only a Victorian could produce: "nowhere in all its course does the American sun behold so high-colored muslins, such flaunting silks and roseate ribbons . . . Such nosegays of hats, such cobwebs of laces, such loves of fans, such shawls, such brocades, such tissues." The merchandise was expensive, but the shops were old and shabby — many of them left over from Spanish times — with the owner and his family living upstairs. Until about 1840, there were no fixed prices; that was a Yankee idea. The Creoles recognized that it was practical and timesaving, but not nearly as enjoyable as haggling and parrying back and forth all morning.

Chartres Street and the other streets near it might have retained their standing if the property owners there had modernized their buildings and charged realistic rents. But many of the Vieux Carré landlords had become absentees, living in France, and they did not understand that times were changing and so was New Orleans. They continued to charge high rents for rundown space until little by little the first-class merchants moved to Canal Street and the American sector, and the French Quarter entered a period of the doldrums that lasted nearly a century.

Canal Street was laid out soon after the American takeover, between the old colonial fortifications and the new American suburb of Faubourg St. Mary, on ground that the French and Spanish had used as a common. Anticipating that a canal would be built there, linking river and bayou (an anticipation since French colonial days), the planners named it Canal Street. The canal was never constructed, but the wide street became a

Right. In ante-bellum days, these shops in the 400 block of Chartres Street were among the city's most fashionable. The entire block was demolished in 1905 to make way for the present Wildlife and Fisheries Building.

VIEW IN CANAL STREET, NEW ORLEANS.

Left. A rare view of Canal Street, made in 1842 by Jules Lion, a free man of color who was one of New Orleans' first daguerreotypists. The three-story building on the near corner was the Bank of Orleans. At the left was the Musson Building, owned by the grandfather of Edgar Degas. The neutral ground (as a wide space down the middle of a street is called in New Orleans) has been planted with young trees, each sapling carefully protected against weather and against any cows and goats that might happen by.

Above. Here is Canal Street as it was in the late 1850s. The hip-roofed house seen at the extreme right of the daguerreotype has disappeared, replaced by part of the Touro Row, which consisted of handsome commercial buildings with iron-lace galleries. Touro Row was begun in 1852 by the tycoon and philanthropist Judah Touro and stood until 1892, when most of it was destroyed by fire. The third Christ Episcopal Church may be seen here one block up the street.

symbol of the distance between the Creoles in the Vieux Carré and the Americans who settled upriver from Canal Street.

The center of the street — which, in New Orleans, is called the neutral ground — was for some time an untended mass of weeds and debris. Here and there an enterprising huckster cleared space for a fruit or coffee stand, but on the whole it was (to quote George Washington Cable) "a place of tethered horses, roaming goats and fluttering lines of drying shirts and petticoats." Both sides of the street were lined with substantial residences, some belonging to doctors, lawyers, or exchange brokers, who used the ground floor of their homes for offices.

One of Canal Street's residents for most of the ante-bellum years was Judah Touro, the richest man in the city. He was born into the small Jewish community in Newport, Rhode Island, and came to New Orleans in 1801 as a nearly penniless young man. He made a large fortune in merchandising, shipping, and real estate, and when he died in 1854 he left most of it to charity. The sum of $10,000 was earmarked for the beautification of Canal Street, whose name was changed by the city council to Touro Avenue. A year later, since people were still calling it Canal Street, the name was officially changed back again. Trees and grass had been planted and the itinerant stall operators dislodged from the neutral ground, but Canal Street did not prove easy to beautify. The English journalist George Sala, visiting in 1885, wrote, "Two rows of trees, grass in the middle. If the grass were green and it were mowed it would be very pretty."

Canal Street's changeover from a residential to a commercial street was accelerated in the early 1850s when Judah Touro built a row of twelve four-story buildings on the downriver side. The Touro Row, as it was called, had cast-iron fronts and cast-iron galleries over the sidewalk. Cast

Top left. By 1890, mulecars and utility poles had appropriated Canal Street's neutral ground and efforts at planting had been temporarily abandoned. The huge tower was a necessary part of the new electric lighting system. Although the local passion for cast-iron galleries had passed its peak, on a rainy day it was still possible to walk along many blocks of the central business district without getting wet.

Left. The Mercier Building was built on Canal Street in 1887, and housed Maison Blanche, one of New Orleans' first department stores. The present Maison Blanche Building dates from 1908–09. It replaced the Mercier Building and gobbled up the space here occupied by the Grand Opera House (with columns) and the other older buildings seen at left.

iron for commercial use was then at the peak of its popularity, in the North and South. It was strong, relatively inexpensive, and lighter than brick or stone. Show windows in a cast-iron front could be much larger than was possible with ordinary construction. Prefabricated sections were shipped by the manufacturer ready to assemble and install, and were available in any of the currently fashionable styles — Greek, Gothic, Italianate, Egyptian, Moorish — designed to imitate wood or stone. The demand for cast-iron fronts, galleries, girders, frames, and ceilings continued through the 1870s. Their demise was partly due to the discovery that they were not as fireproof as had been originally believed (although they didn't burn, they sometimes melted) and partly because of the advent of steel construction. During the peak years, New Orleans' central business district acquired dozens of buildings that used cast iron, some of it imported from the north and the rest from local foundries or from a large ironworks in Holly Springs, Mississippi. Such buildings lasted well and, barring serious fires, would still be standing were it not for the attack of real estate speculation that hit downtown New Orleans in the 1960s and early 1970s. Many handsome and useful buildings in the central business district disappeared at that time.

The first important American architects to leave their marks on New Orleans were Benjamin Latrobe and his son, Henry. The elder Latrobe, born in England in 1764, was an experienced architect when he immigrated to this country in 1796. Not long thereafter he designed the first Greek Revival building in America, the Bank of Pennsylvania, in Philadelphia. He was summoned to Washington in 1803 to complete the national capitol, and again in 1814, to repair and enlarge that building after it had been burned by the British during the War of 1812.

In 1807 he designed a custom house for New Orleans, which was built without Latrobe being on the scene. Unfortunately, he had not allowed for the difficulties presented by the soft soil, and his handsome little Greek Revival custom house was so full of cracks within a decade that it had to be torn down. His contacts with New Orleans in connection with the custom house gave rise to a new scheme — one that would use his engineering talents as well: to supply the city of New Orleans with piped water. In 1811 he sent his eighteen-year-old son Henry to New Orleans to represent his interests. The waterworks project was slow to begin; meantime, Henry, who spoke French and got on well with the Creoles, designed a number of private houses and several public buildings, including the third Charity Hospital, which was later converted for use as the State House.

After the War of 1812, the waterworks finally got underway. Henry Latrobe supervised the construction of an attractive octagonal engine house of his father's design, inspired by the Tower of the Winds in Athens and resembling Philadelphia's waterworks building, which Latrobe had designed some years earlier. On September 3, 1817, while the construction was still going on, young Henry Latrobe died of yellow fever.

Part of this commercial row in the 1800 block of Magazine Street is still standing, but radically changed and minus the engaging row of little dormer windows. Much of the charm of old New Orleans depended on the repetition or similarity of special architectural details, house after house and block after block.

In January 1819, Benjamin Latrobe arrived in New Orleans. His main purpose was to supervise the completion of the waterworks, but he was soon approached about other commissions, including one for a central tower for the cathedral. He liked the city and foresaw a prosperous life there, so he went north and brought back his wife and children. The following September, when the waterworks was nearing completion at last and the architect had completed designs for the Louisiana State Bank, Latrobe died of yellow fever on the third anniversary of his son's death. The bank was built from his designs and still stands.

•

Latrobe missed the golden age of building in New Orleans by a decade. During the 1830s the city acquired several first-class architects, and their influence (and a few of their buildings) can still be seen. The best known of the newcomers was James Gallier, who was born in Ireland in 1798, studied in England, and arrived in New Orleans, after a sojourn in New York, in 1833. For a while he was in partnership with another architect from the north, Charles Dakin; later, each headed separate firms. Charles Dakin, who went into partnership with his brother James, died of yellow fever in 1839 at the age of twenty-eight. Gallier's son, James Gallier, Jr.,

Only these drawings from Jacques Tanesse's city map of 1817 survive to show Benjamin Latrobe's custom house and waterworks.

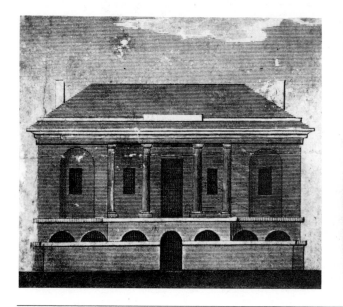

born in 1827, followed in his father's footsteps. Other outstanding architects of the period were Charles F. Zimpel and Henry Howard; among the Creoles, the Frenchman J. N. B. De Pouilly was much in demand. But most New Orleans buildings at that time were the work of contractors and self-taught architects. Despite a lack of formal training, some of these men were very able and coped well with the challenge of making firm foundations in soggy terrain.

The French Quarter was still a prime location as far as the business community was concerned when, in 1836, Charles Dakin and James Gallier were commissioned to build the Merchants' Exchange in Royal Street. The Dakin-Gallier partnership was dissolved soon after, and the Merchants' Exchange was finished by Gallier. The exterior had an almost modern simplicity. In contrast, the interior was elaborate, with Corinthian columns and a very fine dome. (Critics warned Gallier that the dome would not stand, but it did — for a hundred years.) Besides functioning as a commercial exchange, this large building also housed the post office. According to Benjamin Norman's *New Orleans and Environs* (1845), there was an entrance on Royal Street for "letters in the foreign languages

The Merchants' Exchange on Royal Street, designed by Charles Dakin and James Gallier, was one of the handsomest buildings erected in New Orleans during the architecturally rich decade of 1830–40. It is shown here as it was being restored, before a fire destroyed it in 1960.

and for the ladies''; gentlemen seeking domestic mail used another entrance. Also in the building were a bookshop and two reading rooms, the only free library in the city. According to the Manhattaner, Oakey Hall, these rooms were also popular for talking, smoking, and playing chess. "'Change time is at early candle-light," Hall wrote.

By twilight the rooms begin to fill . . . Of all the crowd perhaps not one calls the city his home, from birth or choice. Faces are here upon whom the Exchange gaslights have shone for many a winter; faces, too, that next year you will look in vain to find. All intent on speculation and accumulation . . . you may search the world over to find the science of money-making reduced to such perfection, and become of such an all-engrossing influence as in New Orleans.

The Merchants' Exchange cost $100,000 to build in 1836, and was one of the finest buildings of that building-rich decade. As the hub of commercial activity moved out of the French Quarter, however, the Exchange fell into disuse. The Quarter continued to deteriorate and, by the turn of the century, the once elegant building had become a flophouse, its interior divided by lath and plaster into tiny sleeping cubicles. It had been snatched from the wrecker by preservationists in 1960 and restored for use as a small theater when an arsonist destroyed it.

This imposing bank building at the corner of Iberville and Royal streets was built in 1838. It was first the Union Bank and then the Citizens Bank. It later passed through other incarnations (and mutilations) until it ended its days in the 1950s as the Royal Fur Salon.

Next door to the Merchants' Exchange was the imposing Union Bank (later, the Citizens Bank) at the corner of Iberville and Royal streets. It survived several remodelings over the years, but was finally demolished and replaced by a drugstore.

Not surprisingly, this money-obsessed city had a great many banks. Bankers wanted the kind of building that was likely to inspire trust, awe, and admiration in the depositors. In 1842, the Englishman George Buckingham described New Orleans banks as being "as splendid in all their interior arrangements as they are imposing in their exteriors." He may have been thinking of the Citizens Bank on Toulouse Street, designed by De Pouilly, with a sculptured pediment and six two-story Corinthian columns. Inside, customers awaiting service could admire a painted ceiling attributed to Domenico Canova, a nephew of the famed sculptor, who had come to New Orleans to paint ceilings in the St. Louis Hotel and had remained to become the city's most sought-after artist. The Citizens Bank was behind, and connected to, the St. Louis Hotel. Its fortunes declined with those of the French Quarter, and the building was demolished late in the nineteenth century.

New Orleans had plenty of banks but not many baths, and it must have been a blessing when in the mid-1830s Dakin and Gallier designed the Arcade Baths on Camp Street. Here twenty-four bathtubs were available — not many, considering that by 1840 the population exceeded 50,000. Each bather could luxuriate in a tub full of dark brown Mississippi water, before or after visiting the ballroom, the billiard room, or the coffeehouse that were also in the building. And there were lodging rooms as well. The Arcade Baths were connected by an arcade to the St. Charles Theater and they burned to the ground when the theater burned in 1842.

A more spectacular arcade was the one on Magazine Street, between Gravier and Natchez, designed in 1833 by Charles F. Zimpel for a newly rich businessman named Thomas Banks. It was a long, three-story, Greek Revival building, divided in the middle by a glass-roofed arcade. On the ground floor were offices, restaurants, auction rooms, a bookstore, and shops that sold "fancy goods." On the second floor were billiard rooms and the Washington Armory, and above those were "sleeping rooms for gentlemen." (One gathers that this was not a hotel in the ordinary sense, but that the sleeping rooms were for gentlemen overtaken by weariness due to lingering too long on the other floors. An 1838 guidebook pointed out that "a person may very well pass the whole twenty-four hours under the roof of this edifice, nor desire other means, either of repose, excite-

Left. The Citizens Bank on Toulouse Street was designed by one of the architects of the St. Louis Hotel, J. N. B. de Pouilly, and was built in the mid-1830s. By the 1890s it had reached the depressing state seen in this photograph, and was razed not long after.

Above. This handsome Greek Revival building at the corner of Magazine and Natchez streets was built in the 1830s as the Commercial Bank. Later it became the offices of the Morgan Steamship and Railroad Company, whose emblem appears on the pediment. It was pulled down some decades ago.

Below. Banks' Arcade on Magazine Street was an enormous, many-purpose building, designed in 1833 by Charles Zimpel. The central portion was a three-story-high arcade roofed in glass. Political meetings were often held here, particularly during the Texas Revolution when it was a gathering place for recruits bound for Texas. Parts of the building still stand, but not the central arcade.

ment, pleasure, or food either for mind or body, than can there be obtained.'' If Banks' Arcade was still intact today it would be a national landmark, for there are only a few arcades in the world surviving from the pre-Victorian era when they were popular. (One in Providence, Rhode Island, was saved by determined preservationists.) Parts of the Banks' Arcade are still standing, but not the arcade itself.

•

''The plain fashion of building has almost entirely gone out of vogue,'' commented the *Picayune* in the late 1850s. If the reporter had been able to foresee the Moresque Building, begun in 1859, his story would have been in headlines. Here was the most ornate commercial building yet seen in the south — or, perhaps, anywhere. It had four cast-iron fronts in an intricate Moorish motif, especially made at the Holly Springs, Mississippi, ironworks. The Moresque building was originally intended to have six

---

The Moresque Building, on Camp Street, designed by William Freret, was one of New Orleans' most delightful examples of cast-iron architecture. It burned in 1897.

The New Orleans Cotton Exchange, designed by H. Wolters in 1882–83, was a Victorian extravaganza costing $380,000, the most ornate structure the city had yet seen. Even though Mark Twain wrote that it would be well worth its cost, "for it will breed its species," it remained unique, and in less than forty years was deemed a fit candidate for the wrecker.

Far left. The Sugar and Rice Exchange on Conti Street was an important center of New Orleans' business life. The building, designed by James Freret, was only a few years old when G. F. Mugnier photographed it, circa 1890. It was demolished in 1963.

Left. Thomas Sully was the architect for the Liverpool, London & Globe Building, at the corner of Carondelet and Common streets. One of the first steel-frame multistory structures in New Orleans, it was built in the late 1880s, but lasted only into the 1920s.

Bottom left. The Anheuser-Busch Brewery at Gravier and South Front streets stayed in business during prohibition by ingeniously diversifying — as can be seen by the ice cream sign on the trucks. When New Orleans went back to drinking beer, the company moved to larger quarters.

stories and a ballroom, but the Civil War intervened and the Holly Springs ironworks became a casualty of war. In the late 1860s the building was finished — not as large as originally intended but still attention-getting. It occupied most of the block bounded by Camp, North, and Poydras streets — until it burned in a spectacular fire on April 15, 1897.

The notion of Moorish inspiration for American commercial buildings was soon passé. The popular post–Civil War style was Second Empire, with its mansard roofs and heavy ornamentation, and this was the style of the Cotton Exchange, which went up in the early 1880s. Mark Twain admired it extravagantly: "massive, substantial, full of architectural graces; no shams or false pretenses or uglinesses about it anywhere. To the city it will be worth many times its cost, for it will breed its species. What has been lacking hitherto was a model to build toward, something to educate eye and taste: a *suggester*, so to speak."

The Cotton Exchange was the first commercial structure in New Orleans to have a cellar. The water table was much lower in the 1880s than it had been in colonial times, and building methods had improved. The next step was steel construction, with hundreds of pilings driven yards deep. These made multistoried buildings — and eventually the Superdome — possible. But to make way for them, many distinguished older buildings had to be pulled down, including the Cotton Exchange. By the turn of the century, New Orleans, whose differentness had always been its great distinction, seemed well on its way to looking like any other city.

3

"Elegance, Ease and Some Convenience"

RESIDENCES

"I have no language to describe my wonder on arriving at N. Orleans!" wrote Mrs. Benjamin Latrobe, wife of the architect, soon after a riverboat brought her and her family to New Orleans in the spring of 1820. But she went on:

So different from [what] I expected. Natchez is a vile hole and I expected New Orleans to be like it. How then was I astonished at the appearance of everything . . . My impatience to see our new home made me resolve to wait for no conveyance, but begin our walk, a mile from the City or rather a mile and a half. My head was really confused with the newness of the scene, the whole way between the city and our house being filled up with houses in the midst of large gardens with the river in front. But to describe our residence will be to describe them all, tho' many houses are larger than ours, but all on the same plan . . . Our lot is 360 feet and 64 front, the house is up 16 steps with a Piazza (or Gallery as they call them here) the whole length of the house front and back, there is no entry or passage like our Baltimore houses, but the front is divided into two rooms about 19 feet square with a door leading into each from the Gallery — each door has an inside door half glass when opened forming a window — one room is a parlour, the other is my bed chamber, the back of the house is divided

---

Left. The parlor at 1420 General Taylor, just before the house was demolished in the 1970s.

into *three,* the center is a dining hall; a room at each end of about 14 feet square, one is Julia's chamber, the other is shelved as a store room with a press for house linen . . . thus you have our whole house there being but one story. The yard is very large and covered with grass, the Kitchen standing on one side entirely detached from the house.

But not all the Americans who came to live in New Orleans in those first decades after the Louisiana Purchase were as cheerful as Mrs. Latrobe. They complained of too many ballrooms and coffeehouses, and too few hotels, boarding houses, and Protestant churches. They found the fortifications ridiculous, the jail medieval, and the hospital too small. And they especially disliked the floor plan of Creole houses, which lacked hallways. Never mind that this arrangement allowed for more spacious rooms and for a greater circulation of air; people raised in the Anglo-

---

The house where Benjamin Latrobe and his family lived must have looked much like this one, which stood on the River Road, on the west bank below Algiers. The design of the house, the formal look of the garden, and the cypress-board fence are all typically Creole.

Saxon tradition were rather suspicious of fresh air anyway — they valued privacy more highly. Many of the newcomers were accustomed to row houses and, since these were well adapted to the narrow, deep lots favored by land developers in New Orleans, row houses soon started going up.

Benjamin Latrobe considered these houses ill-suited to a warm climate. He wrote in his diary:

The merchants from the old United States who are daily gaining ground on the manners, the habits, the opinions, and the domestic arrangements of the French, have already begun to introduce the detestable, lop-sided London house, in which a common passage & stairs acts as a common sewer to all the necessities of the dwelling & renders it impossible to preserve a temperature within the house materially different from that of the atmosphere . . . With the English arrangement the red brick fronts are also gaining ground, & the suburb St. Mary, the American suburb, already exhibits the flat, dull dingy character of Market Street, in Philadelphia, or Baltimore Street, instead of the motley & picturesque effect of the stuccoed French buildings of the city. We shall introduce many grand & profitable improvements, but they will take the place of much elegance, ease & some convenience.

From the moment of the Louisiana Purchase, the city was a land speculator's dream. (And even before: some enterprising Americans had anticipated a real estate boom, or had had inside information about its probability, and therefore made fortunes from shrewd New Orleans investments.) Not only was the original section of town, which the Creoles called the Vieux Carré and the Americans called the French Quarter, already crowded, but most newcomers did not want to live there, for it seemed to them peculiar and foreign. Nor were the Creoles inclined to welcome them. However, just upriver from Canal Street there were several desirable tracts that had once been a plantation of the Jesuits. In 1763, the Jesuits had been expelled from Louisiana for political reasons. At that time, their well-cleared and meticulously tended land had been auctioned in six parcels. A large parcel eventually acquired by the Gravier family was subdivided in 1788, creating Faubourg St. Mary, and after the purchase it quickly became the area most favored by the incoming Americans.

Some householders bought two adjacent lots and built detached houses with gardens at one side. The delights of these gardens helped beguile homesick newcomers into forgetting their northern homes. In Creole gardens, the shrubbery was massed just inside the fence (usually a cypress picket fence) rather than under the windows, in the English manner. This scheme was thought to be more healthful as well as cooler. Besides, thick shrubbery at the outer edge of the garden gave more privacy and also

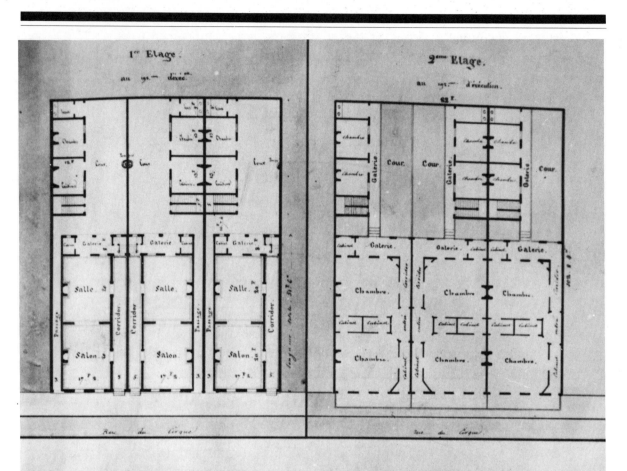

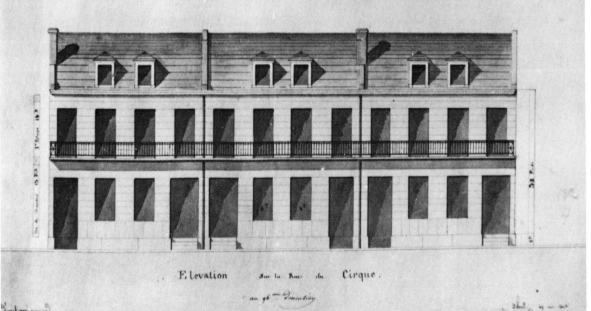

Elevation sur la Rue du Cirque.

subdued some of the street noises and disagreeable odors. The shrubs and trees might be myrtle, orange, oleander, rose, or althea, to name a few. Later in the century, new specimens were added: catalpa, fig, some hardy species of palm, and so many varieties of camelias and azaleas that these flowers are now considered typical of New Orleans. A favorite shade tree was the indigenous live oak, with its graceful drapery of Spanish moss. (The moss was not always purely decorative; it was useful for stuffing mattresses and for filling in chinks between bricks as well as for insulation.) Most Americans took a fancy to the local fashion for formal flower beds outlined with bricks and divided by swept pathways rather than by grass.

On the downriver side of the old town, the Creole planter Bernard de Marigny subdivided his plantation and laid out Faubourg Marigny at about the same time that Faubourg St. Mary was coming into being upriver. A French engineer named Nicolas de Finiels made the plan and it was executed by another French engineer, Bartholemy Lafon. The plan called for two spacious residential avenues, Esplanade and Elysian Fields, and a network of streets that soon became lined with the simple cottages of native-born artisans and workers, including many "free persons of color."

In ante-bellum New Orleans, free persons of color were sometimes relatively well off. If they had white fathers who saw fit to help them, they might even be wealthy enough to own slaves themselves; or they might be taught a skilled craft or be sent to France for a good education. In the 1790s and again in 1804, thousands of free persons of color who were fleeing the slave revolution in Santo Domingo were admitted to New Orleans under a waiver of a law prohibiting nonwhite immigration. These people had skills and they became useful citizens in a city that was always eager for skilled labor. A battalion of free men of color volunteered and fought with Andrew Jackson at the Battle of New Orleans. In 1847, a free man of color invented the vacuum pan, an important improvement in the sugar-refining process that enabled planters to make a greater profit. Free "coloreds" were prominent in the building trades, and it was from their hands that the Creole Faubourgs acquired many of their neat, sturdy

Left. These row house plans, obviously intended for Creole families, are a mixture of French and American ideas. An inside corridor provides separate access to each room, in the Anglo-American fashion. The back-gallery and the separate kitchen are in the tradition of colonial New Orleans.

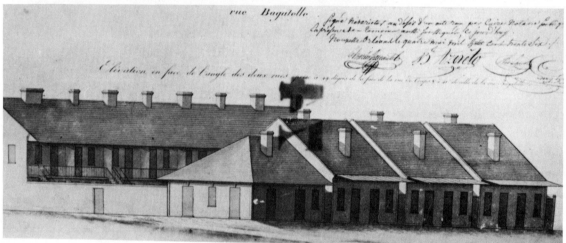

Above. Two-family Creole cottages in Faubourg Marigny. The modest facades of these houses disguised the fact that behind them were large yards, kitchens, and servants' quarters.

Opposite, above. Creole cottages on Bagatelle Street (now Pauger Street) follow the French plan, with no inside passages. The round objects in the courtyards are cisterns.

Opposite, left and middle. The shed roof, an odd style with a cut-in-half look, was often used as a space-saving device in city outbuildings and small cottages.

Opposite, right. A typical cottage on Craps Street. This street, named for a favorite New Orleans pastime, is now merely an extension of Burgundy Street.

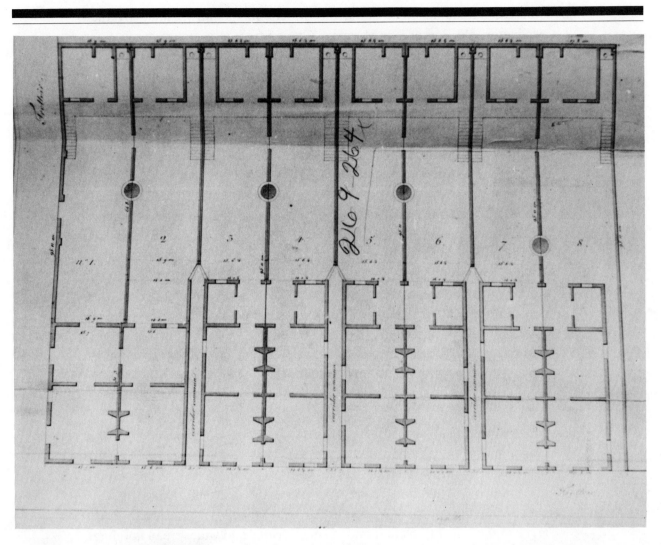

cottages, including those along the streets so quaintly named by their originator, old Bernard de Marigny: Craps Street, Bagatelle Street, Love Street (where, people said, Marigny had a mistress), and Good Children Street. Those engaging street names, along with many houses in this part of New Orleans, no longer exist; the streets having been made extensions of other streets.

The classic Creole cottage had no basement and was built flush with the banquette, or sidewalk, on a foundation of cinders or brick. The interior was a square, divided four ways, without corridors or staircases. The chimney was usually between the two front rooms. Under the gable-ended roof, which overhung the sidewalk, there was an attic, ventilated by dormer windows. An outside passage, entered from the street by way of a gate, led back into a yard and to an outside kitchen at the rear of the lot. Above the kitchen there might be a room or two for slaves, if the owner could afford them. There was also a privy and a cistern. The construction was likely to be brick-between-posts, covered with stucco. Later, wood was commonly used and the house was raised off the ground on brick piers. Greek Revival detail was another later addition, either to embellish new houses or to update old ones.

·

As it became evident that New Orleans was to have a great future, other planters who owned land above the Graviers and below the Marignys hastened to get into the real estate business. The Livaudais plantation, not far above Faubourg St. Mary, suffered disastrous damage in 1816 because of the Macarty Crevasse (so called because of a break in the levee at the Macarty plantation, causing serious and widespread flooding). The Livaudais land was left under several feet of silt. Although silt ruined farmland, it proved advantageous when it came to selling building lots: at sea level, every inch of altitude helps. Madame de Livaudais, née Marigny, sold the land, took her profits of half a million dollars, and went to live in France, leaving behind a large, unfinished house. As the American suburbs grew up around it, children of the neighborhood peeked in the windows and ran when anything creaked. It was a haunted house until it was torn down in 1863.

Whenever a plantation was subdivided, the one-time big house was likely to survive for a time, occupying a lot much larger than the rest. The Saulet house on Annunciation Street, which was built in the 1830s,

The burgeoning city, with its new faubourgs, is shown in this 1817 map by Jacques Tanesse, a French cartographer. The original town, now called the French Quarter, is in the center. The American suburbs — Faubourg St. Mary and the streets laid out by Lafon — are at the left, and the French faubourgs are at the right. The *batture,* along the riverfront, was land built up by the river since New Orleans was founded.

Top left. The eighteenth-century Saulet plantation house was remodeled in the 1830s, when it was given the flat, balustraded roof and the peristyle seen here.

Bottom left. Melpomene, at Carondelet and Melpomene streets, was owned for years by the Bringier family. They built the famous upriver showplace, L'Hermitage.

Above. In 1820, a well-to-do citizen named David Olivier built himself a fine house in the Creole manner, with a hip roof, double galleries, and an outside staircase. Eventually, the house was squeezed in by other buildings on lower Chartres Street. For many years, it was used as an orphanage.

eventually became St. Simeon's Select School. Later it was given to Mercy Hospital, whose board of trustees doomed it to destruction in 1959 by selling it to a supermarket. Melpomene, which stood on Carondelet Street between Melpomene and Terpsichore, was the home of the Bringier family until after the Civil War. It then became a school for freedmen, and later it stood empty. Having gone to rack and ruin along with the neighborhood around it, Melpomene was demolished before the turn of the century.

Rack and ruin, followed by demolition, has been the fate of nearly all the old plantation houses in New Orleans. A celebrated example was the

Olivier house, built in 1820 below the city at the corner of what later became Chartres and France streets. It had already been overtaken by warehouses when it was advertised for sale in 1840: "a beautiful brick dwelling house of two stories; two other brick buildings used for kitchens and servants quarters; stable and coach-house, two brick pigeon-houses, etc." It was bought by the Catholic Church and became St. Mary's Orphan Asylum. Its demolition in 1950, though distressing to lovers of New Orleans architecture, had one happy result: the futile, last-minute effort to save it was an important factor in the founding of the Louisiana Landmarks Society, which has since helped save a number of other important buildings and whose very existence has spotlighted the need for citizen interest in the city's heritage.

A similar case was that of the Delord-Sarpy house on Howard Avenue. Built in 1818 on land that had first belonged to Bienville and later to the Jesuits, it was a fine, hip-roofed plantation house in the French colonial manner, with galleries on three sides, two large, nearly square rooms on each floor, and fine dormers. In the 1950s, the Louisiana Landmarks Society, headed by the architectural historian Samuel Wilson, Jr., led an effort to save it. Wilson wrote, "To preserve this important landmark should be a civic obligation of the people of New Orleans." Had it been restored, it would have been the only authentic plantation house in the center of the city, as well as the oldest building above Canal Street. But other wills prevailed and, in 1957, it was destroyed to make way for a ramp of the Mississippi Bridge.

Of course, the destruction of plantation houses was sometimes unavoidable. They burned down, or the Mississippi took them. A case in point was Avondale, built in 1839 by Senator G. A. Waggaman a few miles above the city, close (too close) to the river. A generation later it was necessary to move the levee back to the very doorstep of the house. Still later, a flood swept Avondale away.

One of the largest and finest of classic plantation houses was that of the De la Ronde family, at Chalmette. In January 1815, during the Battle

---

Top right. Like the Olivier house, the Delord-Sarpy mansion became a victim of city growth and of road-building activities in the 1950s.

Bottom right. Avondale plantation house is seen here as it was about 1875. The river later destroyed it.

of New Orleans, the British used this house as a hospital and, when the fighting went against them, "almost every room was crowded with wounded and dying" (as one of the officers who survived later wrote in his memoirs). The body of the commanding general, Sir Edward Pakenham, was brought there from the field. "Mortifying defeat had again attended the British arms, and the loss in men and officers was frightfully disastrous . . . on all sides nothing was heard but the piteous cries of my

H. Laclotte, an eyewitness of the Battle of New Orleans, later painted this scene of the action at Chalmette Battlefield. (The Macarty plantation house, at left, no longer stands.) The British bravely attacked the American lines again and again, suffering the loss of two thousand men, whereas the Americans had only six or seven killed and about sixty-five wounded. Peace had already been signed in Europe when the battle took place, but news of it had not reached the combatants.

poor countrymen, undergoing various operations . . ." The plantation was sold and subdivided in the 1830s, and the old house deteriorated. According to Samuel Wilson, Jr., this house was "of the first importance in the history of Louisiana architecture." It might still have been restored, even after severe damage from the hurricane of 1915, but instead its ruin was allowed to become irreversible. When Chalmette Battlefield was made a National Historic Park in 1965, these ruins were stabilized. The Beauregard house, another plantation house in pitiful condition, was expertly restored and now serves as headquarters for the National Park Service.

Three Oaks plantation house, near Chalmette, was built in 1831 by a Creole planter, Sylvain Peyroux. Unfortunately, the land on which it stood was acquired in this century by the American Sugar Company, which took no interest in the old house. In June 1965, officials of this company put a stop to the preservationists' protests by having the house bulldozed overnight.

The De la Ronde house, at Chalmette Battlefield, was the home of poverty-stricken tenants when G. F. Mugnier, the New Orleans photographer, took this picture about 1890. The house is now a total ruin.

But in the case of Seven Oaks, across the river in Westwego, even the combined efforts of the Louisiana Landmarks Society and many other preservationists, both organizations and private individuals, were fruitless. Seven Oaks, built about 1840 by the Zeringue family, was once one of the most beautiful plantation houses in Louisiana. It had twenty-six two-story-high Doric columns that completely surrounded the interior in peristyle fashion. This architectural style was once typical of the grandest houses along the river near New Orleans. Now, the nearest one still standing is Oak Alley, fifty miles upriver. The Zeringue family continued to make Seven Oaks their home until 1891, when it was sold for use as a pleasure garden. In 1912, the Missouri Pacific Railroad acquired the property and from then on the house was neglected. Damage from several hurricanes as well as the ravages of vandals and souvenir hunters was never repaired but only pointed to by railroad officials as reasons for tearing the place down. By the 1970s it was a heartbreaking ruin, with vines, grass, and shrubbery sprouting from it as if it were in a Mayan jungle. The interior was a shell, but the lovely columns were still standing. Experts said it was not too late to restore the house, although the cost would be tremendous; or, for far less money, the ruins might have been stabilized and a small park created around them. These suggestions came from many quarters. The railroad was not being asked to put out any money, but only to sell the house and a small acreage around it. But the final fate of Seven Oaks was in the hands of the railroad officials, who, in the summer of 1977, finally took action. First, they made some sanctimonious public pronouncements: the house, unfortunately, was a wreck; it was a hazard to company employees and the Westwego city government had condemned it; the company was eager to contribute to the welfare of the Westwego area by developing the land industrially; the house had no historical significance; and people ought to put their effort and money into something else. With that, the bulldozers arrived and sent Seven Oaks into eternity.

·

As New Orleans grew and the old plantations were subdivided into building lots, it was necessary to find imaginative city planners. Because of the bends in the river and the saucerlike contour of the land, the conventional grid pattern of the original town would no longer suffice. In 1806, Bartholemy Lafon, who had come to New Orleans in the 1790s and had

had experience in laying out Faubourg Marigny, began to devise an ingenious plan for what is now called the Lower Garden District (the area between the Garden District and the central business district).* Some of his plan and most of his extraordinarily named streets (Dryades, Melpomene, Terpsichore, Polymnia, Euterpe, and more) are still extant. Annunciation Square, near the river, became an attractive residential area,

* The boundaries of the Garden District itself are listed in *The National Register of Historic Places* as Carondelet Street, Magazine Street, Josephine Street, and Louisiana Avenue. Some people prefer to substitute St. Charles Avenue for Carondelet Street as the northern boundary and Jackson Avenue for Josephine Street on the east. The term *Garden District* was used as early as the 1850s to designate the elegant section of town where blocks were divided into only four lots, allowing each house to have a spacious garden. There is no Upper Garden District.

Above. Three Oaks plantation house (at far right) was in good condition when this photograph was taken, but it was already in the hands of the American Sugar Company, whose refinery is in the background, and its days were numbered.

Right. A closer view of Three Oaks.

Above. Seven Oaks plantation house in Westwego, photographed shortly before it was razed in 1977. The storage tanks belong to the Missouri Pacific Railroad.

Right. The ruined columns of Seven Oaks.

as did Coliseum Square — although the "great institution of learning" that Lafon intended for it was never built. Tivoli Circle was to be an outdoor pleasure garden, with a circular canal making an island of its center. The pleasure garden never worked out as Lafon had hoped, but the circle is still a circle — Lee Circle — and, beginning in the late 1840s, it was built up with elegant houses, most of them in the Italianate style that was just then coming into fashion. In February 1884, from the balcony of one of these Italianate houses (designed by James Gallier, Jr., and owned by Colonel Augustus May), the two daughters of Robert E. Lee watched the unveiling of a heroic statue of their father. The statue still stands, defiantly facing north, on a pedestal 106 feet high. The pedestal is so lofty that Lee seems to inhabit some exalted sphere, while the circle named for him dwells drearily in the midst of traffic. There is only one house left now; the others have been replaced by three gas stations, several office buildings, and a ten-story YMCA.

Another once-charming residential oasis was Lafayette Square in Faubourg St. Mary, within walking distance of the business district. "It was the resort of citizens of all ages and of all classes," wrote the New Orleanian Henry Castellanos in his book *New Orleans As It Was* (1895). In the morning there were nurses and babies; at noon, school children; in the afternoon, laborers taking siestas; and later, the nurses and children again as well as "staid old denizens," sauntering up and down the foot paths. After dark came "many a Romeo, under the guise of a brawny Celtic drayman" and "a gentle Juliet by his side, who had but just escaped from a neighboring kitchen." Substantial houses faced on the park, which, as in the case of every New Orleans square at that time, was surrounded by a cast-iron fence to keep stray goats and cows from eating the greenery. Nowadays there is no such life for Lafayette Square. The handsome residences are all gone, replaced by characterless office buildings and a hotel. Only the Greek Revival former city hall (now called Gallier Hall, for its architect) still stands — its prestige re-established through the efforts of preservationists and especially of the Louisiana Landmarks Society.

Beyond the streets and squares planned by Lafon were a cluster of riverside villages. In 1833 the three of these nearest the city were incorporated to make the city of Lafayette. Twenty years later Lafayette became part of New Orleans. Its former boundaries now embrace the Garden District, which, in the two decades just before the Civil War, acquired some of the most delightful houses in this — or, indeed, in any other — American city. After his visit to the city in the early 1880s, Mark Twain wrote that domestic architecture there was "reproachless, notwithstanding it remains as it always was . . . These mansions stand in the center of large grounds, and rise, garlanded with roses, out of the midst

---

This Coliseum Street house was built shortly after the Civil War by the owner of the Miller Candy Company (now the Elmer Candy Company). The mixture of detail was typical: two styles of columns, two styles of roof, two styles of window treatment, and two patterns of cast-iron railing. The house was acquired by Touro Infirmary within recent years and has been replaced by a cement block structure.

of swelling masses of shining green foliage and many-colored blossoms. No houses could well be in better harmony with their surroundings, or more pleasing to the eye, or more homelike and comfortable-looking." Mark Twain's judgment is still valid.

Many such houses are still standing, now protected by landmark designations and by a growing public sense of pride. Nevertheless hundreds have been destroyed in recent years and the survivors are far from safe. Mrs. Martha Robinson, a distinguished New Orleanian who has lived more than ninety years in this city, says that it is to her "like lights going out." A letter she wrote not long ago gives a vivid sense of what has taken place during her lifetime.

On the upper river corner of St. Charles and Jackson was the charming home of Mrs. Eastman. It is now a Gulf filling station. Across the Avenue, corner of Jackson, was the Edgar Farrar residence, and next to it the George Whitney

---

Left. Number 2728 St. Charles Avenue is a good example of the houses built by well-to-do New Orleanians in the last quarter of the nineteenth century. This house was originally a raised cottage and was later remodeled. It was razed in the mid-1970s.

Right. Mrs. Charles A. Whitney's Second Empire mansion, with its gardens, stables, and outbuildings, occupied almost an entire block at the lakeside corner of St. Charles Avenue between Jackson Avenue and Philip Street. "No other home in New Orleans has more ground than this one covers," said Jewell's *Crescent City Illustrated.* Built in the early 1870s, its interior decoration reflected the then-fashionable Japanese influence.

The Chaffraix house, which stood at 2833 St. Charles Avenue from 1872 until 1958, was a fine example of one of New Orleans' most attractive house styles, the raised villa.

home and that of Dr. Rudolph Matas — all replaced by large apartment buildings. Between First and Second Streets where the beautiful home of Miss Nellie Farwell stood are three bungalow type cottages, and the Andrew Jackson Apartments occupy the corner of St. Charles and Second, where the handsome Frank Hayne mansion stood. Across the Avenue the home of Judge Erasmus Fenner was replaced by a sort of apartment motel, despite the protests of the neighbors. But the worst blow to the architecture of New Orleans and the character of St. Charles Avenue was the demolition of the uniquely beautiful home of Madame Chaffraix and the splendid home next to it.

On Coliseum was the handsome residence of the Leeds family, and across the street from this was the fine residence of the Hart family, later owned by the Schmidts. On Race Street, the top boundary of Coliseum Square, was the handsome home of Asahel Cooper — now replaced by some modern brick cottages . . . On Prytania Street were the home of Dr. George Pratt and the Richardson house. Many other fine homes on Prytania below Jackson have been demolished

The last owner of this house at 2126 Prytania Street willed it to the Episcopal church as a residence for the bishop. A recent bishop turned it down, and the house has now been replaced by a condominium.

for apartments. Above Jackson Avenue the Garden District Association has been active in protecting their area, but in spite of their efforts the old Stauffer house, corner of Prytania and Jackson, and the old Parker house, owned by Harry McCall in later years, were destroyed and the home of Miss Nellie Henderson, corner of Jackson and Prytania, was replaced by an apartment, as required by her will if the Episcopal Bishop would not use it as his residence.

I have quoted Mrs. Robinson at length, but she could go on in this vein for pages. She could also tell us about a much brighter side of the story. In the last fifteen or twenty years she has seen a growing appreciation for the heritage of New Orleans — so much so that now St. Charles Avenue is protected by a landmarks commission. There are also other preservationist societies all over town: besides the Louisiana Landmarks Society and the Friends of the Cabildo, there are the Preservation Resource

Above, left and middle. The house at 2306 Esplanade belonged to Michel Musson, an uncle of Edgar Degas. In 1871, Degas stayed here for several weeks. The Musson house is still standing, though considerably changed. One quarter of it has been detached and added to a later house, built in what was once the Musson garden. The cast-iron gates and fence are gone.

Above, right. One of four identical houses built on speculation by the architectural firm of Mondelli and Reynolds. One is still standing (928 Euterpe), but altered beyond recognition. This one was on Constance Street. Latticework was often used in New Orleans, but the treatment here is unusual.

Above, far right. The Three Sisters were built in 1834 on Rampart Street by James Gallier. In his autobiography, Gallier wrote, "While living in London, where every inch of building ground is turned to the best account, I had some experience in contriving to make the most of small spaces . . . There were three gentlemen [in New Orleans] who owned, among them, one lot of ground of no very great extent . . . One of them said in a jocular way *he* should like three good houses built upon it. I took the hint, and made a plan for three houses which appeared so feasible that they made a contract with me to build them, and when finished the owners expressed the highest satisfaction and called them the Three Sisters."

Right. This photograph by the late New Orleans architect Richard Koch was taken from a gallery of one of the Three Sisters. They were demolished in the 1960s.

Center, the Vieux Carré Property Owners, Residents, and Associates, the Coliseum Square Association, and more. The barn door is locked now and no more horses can be stolen — or, at least, not easily.

·

The lost houses of New Orleans were in many architectural styles, from French colonial to Beaux Arts, for over the years all the leading styles

were to be found in the city. But the one that predominated and that New Orleans adopted and made its own was Greek Revival. It was widely used for both public and private buildings. It arrived in New Orleans somewhat later than it did elsewhere and it lasted longer.

The most familiar characteristics of a Greek Revival house, of course, are columns, whether Ionic, Doric, or Corinthian, forming a portico or a gallery before the main entrance. The scheme may be found on the

Elevation of adjoining buildings

grandest mansion and on the simplest cottage — the cottage perhaps having as few as three plain columns, five feet or so from the door, whereas the mansion may have a dozen or more soaring columns and two wide galleries, one above the other. These galleries were an important reason for the enduring popularity of the Greek Revival style in New Orleans, since they so admirably suited the climate and the way of life (and are now so forlornly empty, as families stay inside with their television sets and air conditioners). Galleries were already traditional in New Orleans before the coming of Greek Revival, but the majestic Greek columns brought a new feeling of opulence and elegance. Also, narrow lots necessitate narrow houses, and nothing could give a narrow house a more imposing look than tall columns, surmounted by a pediment fit for a temple. These houses were often painted white in imitation of the marble of the ancients (which had, in fact, been painted in vivid colors, but nineteenth-century archeologists did not have that knowledge).

But even houses without columns and galleries, painted gray or yellow, dark red or dark brown, could be called Greek Revival. Many New Orleans row houses were built with pilasters framing their doorways; rectangular transoms (instead of arched, in the Spanish manner); with pedimented gables, simple friezes, and molding designs copied from the Greek. Raised cottages and raised villas became New Orleans' most distinctive regional creation when they were embellished with Greek Revival detail.

·

In the north, Gothic Revival supplanted Greek Revival in popularity, but in New Orleans, Gothic Revival was never much used, except for churches, probably because its typical high-pitched roof and narrow latticed windows tend to retain heat. One exceptional example is the Orange

---

Above, left. A drawing of Union Terrace, four substantial townhouses on Canal Street, designed by James Dakin in the 1830s. The facade on the right was later used for the Grand Opera House (seen in the view of Canal Street on page 172).

Far left. The Waldo house on Broadway, built just after the Civil War for a prominent local publisher, had a one-story gallery across the front and a two-story one in back. The house is gone, but some of the oaks are still standing.

Left. A Greek Revival doorway on lower St. Charles Avenue, photographed on its last day.

Grove plantation house, which still stands, although in ruinous condition, just below the city at a point on the river known as Detour á l'Anglais, or English Turn. It was at this point in 1699, that Bienville encountered an English ship, bound upriver. By pretending to be at the head of vast forces, Bienville persuaded the ship's captain to turn around and leave the Mississippi as fast as possible. The land on which Orange Grove stands was cleared in very early colonial times and became a sugar plantation. In 1850 it was inherited by a Philadelphian, Thomas Asheton Morgan, who proceeded to build a house equipped with such surprising fancies as a basement, a hot-air furnace, and a sewage system. The interior was expensively fitted with marble floors, silver-plated doorknobs, and stained glass. Today all its frills and amenities are gone, but the sturdy Philadelphia brick walls are still standing, and restoration might be possible.

Another Gothic mansion was Harvey's Castle, on the west bank of the river, opposite the city. It was built in the 1840s, but exactly in what year and by whom is uncertain. From about 1848 to 1870 it was the home of a sea captain, Joseph Harvey, and his wife Louisa Destrehan, a Creole heiress. The two owned and operated Harvey's Canal, nearby. Their "castle" had two crenelated towers, narrow windows, and a parapet along the roofline. But the anonymous architect must have been a local man; he could not resist giving his stern Gothic pile the New Orleans touch of a double gallery across the front. After 1870, the building was rented by Jefferson Parish as a courthouse. Later, it became a tenement, and was in an advanced state of dilapidation when, in 1924, it was razed by the federal government in a canal-widening project.

·

Italianate architecture came to New Orleans in the 1840s from the North, by way of England, and was soon embraced by prosperous housebuilders. With its high ceilings and large windows, it was as well suited to the New Orleans climate as to that of Italy; its ornate, palazzo quality pleased the newly rich; and its balconies and cupolas appealed to the high sense of the romantic that was a strong characteristic of ante-bellum southerners.

Left. Orange Grove plantation house, a rare example of residential Gothic Revival in the South, still stands, but it is in desperate need of restoration.

One of the city's most important Italianate mansions was built in 1853 by James Robb, a millionaire who made his fortune during the 1840s as a broker, a banker, and a railroad tycoon. Two stories were planned for the Robb house, but financial difficulties for the Jackson and Great Northern Railroad obliged Robb to settle for one. The one story made a charming miniature palazzo (although not much more Italian than a mint julep). Frescoes adorning the interior have been attributed to Domenico Canova, and the garden was filled with statuary, including a copy of Hiram Powers' *The Greek Slave*. The house stood on part of the old Livaudais property. Robb was soon obliged to sell the place to another and more fortunate tycoon, John Burnside, who occupied it until his death in 1881. Burnside furnished and decorated the house lavishly. "A bijou of comfort," was the way a lady visitor, Mrs. Julia LeGrande, described it. In 1890, the mansion became Sophie Newcomb College and acquired a second story. Later, it was the Baptist Bible Institute. It was razed in the 1950s and replaced by small houses.

Among many outstanding examples of the Italianate style was the Esplanade Avenue house built in the 1850s by Hamilton M. Wright, a Yankee merchant who became a staunch Confederate. Later it belonged to the Slocomb family, and then, for many years, to the Roman Catholic archdiocese as a residence for the archbishop. Its place has now been taken by a used car lot. The Campbell house, at the corner of St. Charles and Julia streets, was perhaps the finest private residence in the city — or, at least, General Ben Butler thought so, since he chose to live in it during his tour of duty as head of the Union occupation forces. At that time it was almost new, having been built in 1859 by the architect Lewis E. Reynolds. After suffering the disfigurement shown in the photograph, the Campbell house was demolished in 1965. Another notable Italianate house

---

Top left. Harvey's Castle, across the river in Algiers, was another Gothic Revival effort. For years it was a landmark for river travelers.

Top middle and right. In the early 1850s, James Robb, a self-made millionaire, bought the block bounded by Camp, Chestnut, and Sixth streets and Washington Avenue, and began to build an Italianate villa. It was his intention to make it, inside and out, the most beautiful house in New Orleans, but he suffered financial reverses and never added the second story. That was done in the 1890s when the house became well known as the home of H. Sophie Newcomb College.

Left. One of the handsomest of New Orleans' many Italianate houses was the Wright-Slocomb house on Esplanade Avenue.

was that of Colonel George Soulé, who built his house in 1869 on St. Charles Avenue. Before doing so, he moved his old house from this spot to a lot about half a block away, where it still stands, having outlived the newer one. House moving was not difficult in New Orleans, since there were no cellars and the ground was level.

It was not long before Italianate features were borrowed by builders of cottages intended for the working classes. Decorative brackets and window moldings, cupolas and balconies gave an important air without great expense. And even before the nationwide architectural eclecticism of the latter third of the nineteenth century, New Orleans builders and home-owners had no objection to mixing styles in one house. For one thing, there was a shortage of trained and authoritative architects who could look a client in the eye and say, "No, you can't do that" or "It isn't

Left. The Campbell house at 805 St. Charles Street was costly and elaborate, but un-lucky. First, it was occupied by the Union general Ben Butler during the Civil War, and then, much later, it was divided into grubby shops downstairs and apartments upstairs. Its finely detailed carriage house (in background at extreme right) still remains and serves as a shelter for attendants at the parking lot that has replaced the house.

Right. The Soulé house at St. Charles Avenue and Eighth Street was Italianate with Second Empire features as well.

done.'' The result was the endless slight variation of style and the faintly amateurish look that gives so much charm to New Orleans streets. "I'd like a house like Mr. So-and-so's," a prospective homeowner might say to his builder "but with Doric pillars, not Corinthian, and a box pediment. Give me a turret, and instead of wooden rails on the gallery I'd like cast iron in the bunch-of-grapes pattern."

•

By 1860, cast iron was as popular in the private sector as it was in the commerical. Prefabricated cast-iron balconies, fences, gates, hitching posts, washstands, garden ornaments, fireguards, and many other domestic items could now be bought from catalogues. They were cheaper than wrought iron, and stronger and easier to maintain than wood. If painted (usually black, but sometimes green, bronze, or cream), they required no care other than an occasional repainting. When such products first came in, they had to be ordered from New York or Philadelphia, but New Orleans foundries were soon producing similar or better ones. In fences

In about 1895, a visiting photographer from New England caught this turbaned "mammy" as she walked along St. Charles Avenue, near Felicity Street. Behind her is an Italianate mansion and a painted cast-iron fence protecting its garden.

and galleries, there was a wealth of patterns to choose from, ranging from simple railings to elaborate designs showing flowers, fruit, vines, or female figures. Fences in the cornstalk pattern were popular and some house-holders painted them yellow and green. (One such fence in the French Quarter is now a tourist attraction and there is another, handsomer, cornstalk fence around a house at Fourth Street and Prytania.) The vogue for decorative cast iron reached its height in the mid-century years. By 1880 it was going out of fashion in most places, but not in New Orleans. Iron lace and New Orleans had become an immortal combination.

In the ante-bellum years, prefabricated house frames (called balloon frames) were also used extensively in New Orleans, as builders hurried to keep up with the rapidly increasing population. A popular local post-Civil War invention was the Louisiana Cottage, a small prefabricated unit, complete with jigsaw decoration, which was shown at the Paris International Exposition of 1867. A company called the Louisiana Steam Sash Blind & Door Factory sold prefabricated jigsaw work of all kinds — brackets, bargeboards, turned-wood columns, and the like — and these were enthusiastically taken up by builders and renovators all over town.

·

New Orleans' most prolific decade, as far as building was concerned, was the 1830s. "The progress of architecture in this city is really astonishing," wrote one resident, in 1833, after returning to New Orleans from a journey. "The number of edifices reared during an absence of eight months is almost incredible." There was an atmosphere of cheerful chaos, like that in a frontier town (and, until the settlement of Texas and the annexation of New Mexico and Arizona, New Orleans was on the southwest frontier). Shacks were replaced in a few months by grand mansions, and formal gardens bloomed where only a year before people had been shooting alligators. There was never a day in New Orleans without the sound of many hammers and saws and the trundling of huge drays in the streets, bearing loads of household furniture.

The financial panic of 1837 slowed but did not halt the growth of the city. There were bankruptcies, and important pieces of property changed hands, but by the early 1840s the hectic rush was on again. And, despite a decline in the city's fortunes, the final ante-bellum decade witnessed the construction of some of its most impressive private dwellings. To use Latrobe's phrase, they provided "elegance, ease and some convenience."

Among well-to-do New Orleanians, the ease and convenience of daily life was considerably enhanced by the presence of household slaves. The usual complement for a prosperous city family was from three to eight servants (they were always called servants, never slaves). House servants were envied by their brethren who were laborers in the field or town, but they were subject to long hours, many irksome restrictions, and the constant threat of corporal punishment. (If their owner was too kind-hearted to whip slaves who had displeased him, they could be sent to the parish prison for a professional job.) Latrobe wrote that he moved out of his boarding house because he disapproved of the constant whipping of the chambermaid, and added that he could not see the white arms of the Creole ladies in the ballroom without picturing them wielding a cowhide whip. The Creoles, on the other hand, insisted that the American women were the cruel ones. In truth, cruelty was not often perpetrated by owners, but was inherent in the system itself. Because of fears of insurrection, more and more restrictive laws were passed to keep blacks in order. By 1859, they were not allowed to learn to read or write, to hold church assemblies, to be legally married, or to move about the city without passes.

Although there was a tremendous gap between slave and master, certain discomforts due to climate and sanitation were suffered by both. The wind from the river brought with it an almost insufferable smell from the slaughterhouses along the waterfront — as well as the offensive essences of soap boiling, tanning, and fertilizer, all offshoots of the slaughtering industry — which permeated the Garden District, despite its elegance. Not until after the Civil War were abattoirs and their satellite factories moved elsewhere.

Even as late as the 1920s, Sherwood Anderson called New Orleans "a city of smells." He wrote, "It reeks with smells from the earth, the sea, the river, the houses, the markets, the swamp. In the moist heavy air the smells hang all day and all night, but in Southern stories nothing is mentioned but the magnolia . . . " If in 1926 the streets were noticeably full of smells other than magnolia, one can imagine what they must have been like before they were paved and before the installation of sewers. Ida Pfeiffer, an English world traveler, wrote in 1856, "I was continually obliged to hold my handkerchief to my face. The people of New Orleans are by no means exact as to where they throw filth and just as often as not find the street most convenient."

Until the 1890s, ninety percent of the streets remained unpaved. There were wide, deep gutters, lined with stone and bridged at intervals by granite slabs. But in a heavy rainstorm, the gutters inevitably overflowed and pedestrians had no choice but to wade. "After a rain . . ." wrote Captain Hamilton, in 1833, "the centre of the street is at least a foot thick of mud, through which foot passengers, when desirous of crossing must either wade up to their knees or set off on a wild goose chase after stepping stones, perhaps a mile distant, which enable them — if they can jump like a kangaroo — to get over dry shod." More than one New Orleanian, writing of the old days, remembered learning to swim in a convenient gutter. And Daisy Breaux Calhoun, a belle of the eighties, wrote that on a rainy evening her mother had slipped while descending from her carriage at the opera and had gone down in the gutter up to her neck.

For those who had no carriages, there was a mule-drawn omnibus — "the Temple of Equality" was what the English journalist George Sala called it, because it was used by everyone. Five cents — a picayune — was the price of a ride, whether short or long (and it could not have been priced lower, because the picayune was the smallest coin in circulation). Few people walked if they could ride, given the condition of the streets, but the sensations of riding were not pleasurable. In 1849, an Englishman named Davies reported "such a course of jolting as we had never before experienced. It seemed as if all the gutters and splash-holes in the universe had been collected together and we had to drive over the whole."

But at least the main streets were gas-lit at night and had been since the 1830s. The gas flames were in square lanterns, suspended on ropes or chains above the middle of the main streets. Lesser streets were lit by oil. "At night a row of these burning lamps," wrote a newcomer from Virginia, "may be seen a mile long." Despite the drawbacks, most visitors found much to beguile them in the cosmopolitan air of New Orleans street life. "French sounds and French smells," observed the landscape architect Frederick Law Olmsted, adding that he had a cab driver who said, "*Oui, yer 'onor*."

"Yer 'onor" indicated the presence of the Irish, and present they were in great numbers, from the early 1820s onward. Together with the Germans, they drastically changed the makeup of New Orleans' working class. In the earlier years, hard labor was performed by blacks, whereas the skilled trades were in the hands of Creoles and free persons of color. Then came the Irish and German waves of immigrants. The Irish were nearly always untrained and very poor. Under British rule they saw no future for themselves at home, and they were desperate, willing to do the most menial and hazardous tasks. Many died digging the canals of New Orleans. Employers preferred them to slaves, because they entailed no legal responsibility and when they died there were always others waiting for their jobs. The Irish actor Tyrone Power, visiting New Orleans in 1836, was appalled by the conditions in which he found his compatriots who were working on the New Basin Canal. He wrote:

I only wish that the wise men at home who coolly charge the present condition of Ireland upon the inherent laziness of her population could be transported to this spot, to look upon the hundreds of fine fellows labouring here beneath a sun that at this winter season was at times insufferably fierce, and amidst a pestilential swamp whose exhalations were foetid to a degree scarcely endurable even for a few moments; wading amongst stumps of trees, mid-deep in black mud, clearing the spaces pumped out by powerful steam-engines; wheeling, digging, hewing, or bearing burdens it made one's shoulders ache to look upon; exposed meantime to every change of temperature in log-huts, laid down in the very swamp . . . Here they subsist on the coarsest fare . . . and all this for a pittance that merely enables them to exist, with little power to save, or a hope beyond the continuance of the like exertion . . . Here too were many poor women with their husbands . . . Such are the labourers I have seen here, and have still found them civil and courteous, with a ready greeting for the stranger inquiring into their condition, and a quick jest.

Most of the Irish settled in the vicinity of Tchoupitoulas Street, in Faubourg St. Mary, and in Lafayette, where the population grew to 15,000 by 1850. The area where they lived, which included some terrible slums, was called the Irish Channel. Some say it was called that because it was often flooded and others say that when Irish seamen coming upriver saw the lights of a certain bar in that neighborhood, they said, "There's the Irish Channel."

The Germans were likely to have at least a rudimentary education and perhaps a skill. Especially during the German political unrest of the 1840s, New Orleans acquired skilled artisans and craftsmen — brewers, bakers, metal workers, shoemakers — as well as a few doctors, lawyers, and teachers. They settled in Carrollton and Lafayette; in Algiers, across the river; and in Faubourg Marigny, which came to be nicknamed Little Saxony. Nearly 54,000 Germans came to New Orleans between 1820 and 1850, and about 25,000 more during the 1850s.

Some of the immigrants from Germany were Jewish, including the first member of the distinguished Warburg family to come to America. Other Jews came from the North, and over the years they made a contribution to the business and cultural community far out of proportion to their numbers. Perhaps the best-known name was that of Judah P. Benjamin, who came from New England in the 1840s and married into a Creole family — as many of his coreligionists did. Benjamin made a large fortune, built a fine plantation house, Belle Chasse, and became a senator from Louisiana. A firm supporter of the Confederacy, he was Confederate secretary of the treasury. After the war he went to live in England, where he became a member of the Bar and practiced law. Belle Chasse, like so many other beautiful houses, fell on evil times. In the early 1920s it was acquired by an association similar to the Mount Vernon and the Monticello associations, which hoped to restore it, but the plan did not succeed. The house was then turned over to Tulane University, which sold it to a private owner. After suffering serious vandalism, Belle Chasse was finally torn down in the 1960s.

After 1865, both the Irish and the Germans continued to arrive, but they were now joined and quickly exceeded in number by Italians. The newest arrivals found living space in the dilapidated houses of the Vieux Carré. A few old Creole families continued to occupy ancestral homes, but the majority had either died off or gone to live in one of the Creole faubourgs. A kind of urban inertia prevailed in the Quarter, which made a slum of many beautiful old houses but preserved them from being demolished.

The poorest immigrants and freedmen went to live on that side of the city known as lakeside, woods side, or simply back of town — a wilderness of swamp and bayou long after it became an official part of the city. For years it was probably the sole place in the United States where it was possible to become lost in unexplored territory within city limits. Thomas Wharton, an architect from the North who moved to New Orleans during the 1850s, had this to say about "back of town":

Plank roads at intervals are pushed far into the swamp — but the banquettes cease and wooden gunwales and planks take their place — the gutters filled with green stagnant ooze and the tenements jostle each other and are graced with innumerable stores of empty barrels, dilapidated wash tubs, remnants of ancient costumes and old and new garments flaunting from the clothes lines — children and dogs without stint clustered around the gateways and from within the yards, alleys, open doors and windows issued fragmentary specimens of every language spoken under the canopy of heaven.

After 1850, the houses of working people were likely to be the type known as *shotgun.* A shotgun house was only one-room wide, and long

This detail of a destroyed house in the Garden District shows the sort of jigsaw ornamentation that once flourished everywhere in New Orleans.

Above. Early examples of shotgun houses, probably built as rental units, on St. Andrew Street. Small though they are, they have been dignified by three square columns apiece. Later examples nearly always had lots of jigsaw work.

Below. The Keller house: a glorious potpourri of architectural styles.

and narrow, with the rooms arranged one behind the next. Although this plan suited the 30- by 120-foot lots usual in working-class neighborhoods, it was not invented for them, but for the slave quarters of plantations. Speculators devised the double shotgun, which housed two families, and, later, the camelback, a uniquely New Orleanian house with a second story above the rear part.

·

After the Civil War, New Orleans acquired its share of the architectural styles fashionable in other parts of the country, but because of the struggles of the Reconstruction period, new houses came later than elsewhere and not in great numbers. Instead of tearing down their Greek Revival or Italianate residences, people made do with them or updated them a bit. All the usual High Victorian styles were represented: mansard roofs, heavy dormers, asymmetry, contrasting scale and texture, brackets, beveled and etched glass, and what architects of the time termed "calculated restlessness."

The mansard roof, which made it possible for multistoried houses to have higher, airier top stories or attics, was the hallmark of the Second Empire style — often called General Grant (though not in the South) because under Grant's administration many new Washington buildings were given this style. The mansard roof was well suited to the New Orleans climate, and a great many sprouted up during the late 1860s and the early 1870s, sometimes capping a new house and sometimes added to an old one. The Keller house at 3453 Magazine Street was a splendid example of the period. It had a little bit of everything: a mansard roof, Corinthian columns, the façade of a raised cottage, an asymmetrical bay window, a Greek Revival doorway, brackets, stained-glass windows, black marble mantels, a widow's walk, and a cupola. In its heyday it also had cast-iron dogs on the lawn. During its last twenty-five years, it served as the mother house of the Eucharistic Missionaries of St. Dominic. In the 1960s it was razed to make way for a more appropriate looking convent.

Thomas Sully was the leading architect in New Orleans during the last quarter of the nineteenth century and the early years of the twentieth. His many houses included examples of Second Empire, Queen Anne, stick-style, shingle, and Romanesque as well as the various revivals — Colonial,

Beaux-Arts, and what might be termed Greek-Revival-Revival. Upper St. Charles Avenue was now the most fashionable part of the city, and Sully houses helped to give it an air of comfortable elegance.

A mixture of styles in one building, sometimes called picturesque eclecticism, characterized the period everywhere in the United States. But in

A house by the architect Thomas Sully at 1137 Esplanade, photographed inside and out just before the wreckers arrived.

Top left. A view on Esplanade Avenue in 1895. The mansard-roofed house has been demolished, but its twin (extreme left) remains.

Top middle. Scalloped shingles, Romanesque arches, and Eastlake pillars were features of the Pokorny house, 2113 St. Charles Avenue.

Top far right. Another Thomas Sully house, which stood until recently at 1828 Palmer. About the time it was built, at the turn of the century, a local magazine noted, ''For $4000 a person can put up a home with art glass windows, first-class plumbing, electric bells and lights, speaking tubes, cast-iron enameled bathtubs, inside blinds, tiled hearths, hardwood mantels, four good bedrooms, parlor, diningroom, library, reception hall, large galleries, kitchen, butler's pantry, and all fencing, paving, etc.'' This residence included most of these amenities.

Right. When this picture was taken on lower St. Charles Avenue during a Confederate parade in 1904, one could walk for blocks in this part of New Orleans and pass nothing but harmonious rows of galleried houses. Now, not only the Confederate veterans are no more, but also every house seen here along their line of march.

Below. Number 3607 St. Charles Avenue was designed by Thomas Sully in about 1890 for the prominent New Orleans businessman Isidore Newman. It was a splendid Romanesque pile that had the durability of a castle. Yet here it is in its last moments, as the wreckers closed in on it in 1972.

Right. The streetcar still runs along St. Charles Avenue, from Canal Street to Carrollton, the last of its kind in the city and one of the last in the country. And the live oaks still arch above the pavement, but less gracefully than they did in the early 1920s, when this photograph was taken. They have had to be pruned to allow tall trucks to pass.

the Crescent City, added to all the conventional fashions of the day, there was nearly always some emphasis, some inspiration, or some eccentricity that proclaimed itself to be pure New Orleans. Greek Revival and Italianate characteristics were fearlessly mixed with any (or all) of the later styles. After all, they were tried and true and so there was no reason to discard them just because they were old-fashioned. Besides, they provided a pleasing nostalgia for ante-bellum days.

C. M. Nichols, an English memoirist, wrote in 1872 about life in New Orleans in 1859, "There was at this period a charm in the life and society of New Orleans, difficult to understand and impossible to describe. 'No place like New Orleans' was the verdict of all who had lived there long enough to know what it was."

"A Palace for Creature Comforts"

HOTELS

When newcomers began to flock to New Orleans after the Louisiana Purchase, they found few hotels to welcome them. One, the Orleans, on Chartres Street, had a hundred beds and twice that many seats at table. If the Orleans was booked up, an alternative choice might well have been a boarding house or the home of an impecunious widow who took paying guests. For single men whose lives were focused on moneymaking, such arrangements usually proved adequate. But an Englishwoman, Mrs. Basil Hall, writing of the boarding house where she stayed with her husband and small daughter in 1828, complained of the service, the beds, the food, and the mosquitoes. She considered the dinner hour — three-thirty in the afternoon — to be "barbarous," and also objected to meals "swallowed in public amidst the clatter of thirty pairs of knives and forks." There was plenty to eat — two courses of meat and vegetables, followed by pies, custards, and fruit — but Mrs. Hall would have preferred less food more fastidiously presented. Her point of view was that of most foreign visitors, who seldom spoke favorably of American boarding houses, North

The first St. Charles Hotel, designed by architects Gallier and Dakin, which was destroyed by fire only fifteen years after it was built.

or South. However, the overcrowding in New Orleans probably made the situation worse.

Visitors with letters of introduction might have managed to stay in a private home; but most transients were single men who had come from the north or from Europe without connections or prospects, determined to become rich or to die in the attempt (and that was no empty cliché, for thousands of these lone fortune seekers died of yellow fever, cholera, and other swift and ferocious diseases, far from their kindred).

The great building boom of the 1830s at last provided New Orleans with the hotels it needed. The construction of large, heavy buildings on soft soil was still imperfectly understood, and one hotel, Planters, went up and then very suddenly came down again. It collapsed during the night of May 20, 1835, burying sixty people in the wreckage. Of these about a

Left. The Orleans Hotel (at right) on Chartres Street was one of the city's first hotels. It was built before 1800 and survived for over a hundred years. On the left was the fifty-room mansion of Samuel Moore, an American businessman, built in the last days of the Spanish regime.

Right. The Planters Hotel toppled down on a May night in 1835. This is an impression by N. Currier, of Currier & Ives, of that event. Disaster prints sold well.

third died. The others, as the bilingual newspaper *L'Abeille* put it, were recovered by firemen, "*respirant encore, mais plus ou moins utiles.*" It appeared that some wooden columns, not reinforced, had broken under the weight of the floors they supported. *L'Abeille* reported that "the building had been for some time of a tottering condition . . . Only the day previous [the owner] had propt one side of the house, but unfortunately neglected the other, although cautioned to do so by a carpenter to whom he applied for advice."

This story demonstrates the happy-go-lucky way in which New Orleans was then run. *L'Abeille* suggested that there might be a need for a building code, adding that builders should be obliged to indemnify victims of careless construction, but nothing much was done about these matters for years.

In 1835 the architects James Gallier and Charles Dakin were asked to build, for a private corporation, a hotel that was to surpass in size and splendor any other in the world. The Gallier-Dakin partnership was dissolved later the same year, and the St. Charles Hotel (so called because it faced on St. Charles Street, just above Canal) established Gallier's reputation and was therefore worth it to him, even though he was paid only $10,000 for three years' work. The total cost of the hotel came to $600,000, exclusive of furnishings, which added up to an additional $150,000.

As Gallier wrote in his memoirs, the assignment was "very arduous and onerous." During the first summer he lost scores of his workmen from sunstroke and yellow fever. Besides, he added, he "was forced to act not only as the architect, but also as clerk of the works and foreman-mechanic in each of the trades engaged in the building, as the only men who could at that time be had knew little or nothing of building beyond the most common structures."

The St. Charles was certainly no common structure. It was taller than any building in New Orleans — six stories, surmounted by a gleaming white dome that could be seen for miles up and down the river. According to Norman's 1845 guidebook, "The effect of the dome upon the sight of the visitor, as he approaches the city, is similar to that of St. Paul's, London." Mr. Norman, beside himself with admiration, went on to speak of the "indescribable effect of the sublime and matchless proportions of this building upon all spectators — even the stoical Indian and the cold and strange backwoodsman, when they first view it, are struck with wonder and delight."

Gallier, a devotee of the Greek Revival style, borrowed the idea of a portico of Corinthian columns from the Hotel Tremont in Boston; but he gave the St. Charles a raised main floor. The raised and recessed portico gave hotel guests a place to stroll without having to go into the dirty street. After dinner, wrote Oakey Hall, there was always "a large tooth-picking crowd" assembled on the portico and the steps of the St. Charles.

In the center of the street-level floor was an octagonal barroom that could — and often did — accommodate one thousand drinking men. The St. Charles bar became a home-away-from-home for prosperous bachelors. "Many a Man-about-town lived nearly altogether at this, or at other bar-rooms," Gallier wrote, "and frequently cut short his life by habits of intemperance, first acquired and afterwards kept up by establishments of this description." Oakey Hall reported that the St. Charles bar was crowded, day and night, except in August, "when Yellow Jack comes into town, and the room echoes to the tread of some score or so, whom death nor disease can not frighten . . ."

Also on the hotel's lower floor were shops, auction rooms for goods and slaves, and public baths. The main floor above was divided into a central salon, dominated by Ionic columns and a marble statue of George Washington; a gentlemen's dining room (called, in those days, an ordinary), which measured 129 feet long by 50 feet wide and had a 22-foot ceiling; a smaller ordinary for ladies; a gentlemen's sitting room; a ladies' parlor, and a ballroom said to be one of the handsomest in the country. The separate facilities for ladies and gentlemen did not mean a monastic segregation of the sexes. Although no ladies were permitted in the gentlemen's public rooms, husbands and invited single gentlemen might mingle in those for ladies. This situation prevailed in most hotels of that time.

"Or it is a winter's evening, and in the ladies' drawing room flash beams of beauty, and gas, and jewels," wrote Mr. Hall, in his charmingly overblown manner.

Here . . . is the modest beauty from Ohio (papa in the pork trade); there a dashing belle, whose altars at Saratoga and the Sulphur-Springs are yet warm with sacrifices of her last summer admirers (her third winter at New Orleans and no husband yet). In yonder corner a red-cheeked, blue-eyed miss from New England (her grandparents snugly in bed the while, in the old homestead, and little dreaming of the — to them — degenerate conduct of their descendant) . . . There will be music, dancing, nonsense, eating, and flirting until three o'clock in the morning, and — the same things for three or four months thereafter.

In the octagonal space under the dome, a spiral staircase led up to the three floors of bedrooms and suites that accommodated five hundred guests. The rooms were reached from galleries on each level, or from corridors that rayed out from the central octagon. There was a circular walk, or gallery, around the top of the dome, and every tourist made a point of toiling up to it, there to look out over the teeming little city, the great brown river with its heavy traffic of steamboats and sailing ships, and the swampy horizons in every direction.

Among the many travelers who stayed at the St. Charles and recorded their impressions of it, very few had unfavorable comments to make. One thrifty New Englander objected to the prices, and a traveler from the British Isles deplored the service, which was largely provided by Irish or German immigrants, fresh from the ship. But, in the 1840s, George Buckingham, a fastidious British visitor, said that the St. Charles seemed to him "the largest and handsomest hotel in the world." And Mrs. Houstoun, author of *Texas and the Gulf of Mexico, or Yachting in the New World,* described her room as "very comfortable, well carpeted, excellent fires, luxurious furniture and curtains of the richest blue damask. The only hotel to which I can at all compare it, is that of 'Les Princes' at Paris . . . My bed room was delightful: such snow-white musquito curtains and endless rocking chairs and Psyches!" (A Psyche was a Grecian-style settee, very much in vogue in the 1840s.)

This splendid pile lasted a bare fifteen years. In the spring of 1851 a fire that started in the kitchen spread through defective chimney flues and within three hours the entire hotel was in ashes. Fortunately the fire occurred in the daytime and no lives were lost. Frederika Bremer, the Danish author of *Homes of the New World,* happened to be visiting New Orleans at that time and wrote that a friend of hers staying at the St. Charles had "early that morning seen a volume of black smoke issue from under her bed. She gave the alarm and sent a message to the master of the hotel, who replied that there was no danger . . . all would soon be put to rights. An hour afterward smoke was again in the room." This time, Miss Bremer's friend decided to leave and it was none too soon. The Danish visitor was impressed that even before the blackened wreckage was cold, a subscription was being circulated to erect another St. Charles. "American expedition!" she noted.

Perhaps it was as well that the St. Charles burned down before it fell down. According to a contemporary architect (not Gallier) the foundations

Top left. The ruins of the first St. Charles Hotel, which burned to the ground in three hours in early 1851.

Bottom left. The second St. Charles Hotel on St. Charles Street, designed by Isaiah Rogers and George Purvis in 1851 and destroyed by fire in 1894.

Above. A G. F. Mugnier photograph of St. Charles Street, with the second St. Charles Hotel in the distance. The building in the foreground is still there, but the urns that ornamented the roof are not. They have made their way to the Bultman Funeral Home at Louisiana and St. Charles avenues, where, painted black, they strike a suitably mournful note.

had settled at least twenty-eight inches, the external walls were cracked, and the floors were "very undulating." At any rate, a second St. Charles Hotel, designed by Isaiah Rogers, the architect of Boston's Hotel Tremont, and George Purvis, was ready for occupancy in less than two years. It was very much like the first, but lacked the impressive great dome. The furnishings were even more elaborate and included five mirrors in the ladies' parlor that were said to be the largest ever imported into the United States. The gentlemen's ordinary was bigger than ever and had five chandeliers. Most of the "elegantly carpeted" bedrooms contained furniture of carved and highly polished black walnut, the latest fashion. Hot and cold running water was another new wrinkle, although it did not run on the upper floors, but only in the baths, which were located in the basement. The water was heated by a steam engine, which, according to one visitor, shook the whole building.

The second St. Charles lasted until 1894, when it, too, burned to the ground. Even in its last days it was still being praised. In 1885, the British journalist George Sala declared that no other American hotel "can equal the architectural magnificence of the exterior of the St. Charles; with its clustered Corinthian columns and great open loggia where you can sit and smoke and gaze upon the scene of almost incessant bustle and activity in St. Charles Street below you."

In 1896, the third St. Charles arose on the same site, a fine, substantial hotel, although hardly remarkable in a world where deluxe hotels had become commonplace. For about sixty years it was a New Orleans favorite for Mardi Gras balls, coming-out parties, high-level political meetings, and as a rendezvous for the elite, to whom it was the equivalent of New York's old Ritz-Carlton. For no imperative reason, the third St. Charles was demolished in 1974. The ghosts of three memorable buildings now hover above a parking lot.

·

While the first St. Charles was under construction, the French Quarter was acquiring its own deluxe hotel, the St. Louis. Two French architects, the brothers Jacques Nicholas Bussière De Pouilly and Joseph Isidore De Pouilly, had won a contest for the best plan, and their creation was very

---

Top right. After the second St. Charles Hotel burned in 1894, it was succeeded by yet another hotel of the same name, which opened in 1896 and was demolished in 1974.

Right. The third St. Charles: an elaborate ironwork elevator cage and stair rail. (The second St. Charles had had the first passenger elevator in New Orleans.)

Far right. The main lobby of the third St. Charles.

handsome and very French, looking as if it belonged on the rue de Rivoli. At that time, relations between the Creoles and the Americans were particularly unfriendly. Indeed, in 1836, the city government divided itself into three municipalities in order to keep quarreling factions separated. New Orleans now had 40,000 transients a year, many of whom were Creole planters from rural Louisiana and "foreign French" businessmen from France. It seemed important not only to offer them accommodations that would remind them pleasingly of Paris, but would also keep them out of bars and coffeehouses where quarrels with the Americans might lead to tombstones that read "*Mort sur le champ d'honneur.*"

On the corner of St. Louis and Chartres streets there had been a merchants' exchange called Hewlitt's (formerly Maspero's), where all kinds of merchandise, inanimate and human, had changed hands daily. Hewlitt's was pulled down when the new hotel, whose lower floor was designed to be used as a new exchange, was nearly completed. The St. Louis (or City Exchange Hotel, as it was often called by the non-French population) opened in January 1838, although the facade, the baths, and the ballroom were not yet finished. Two years later it burned down, with a loss of several lives. It was promptly rebuilt.

Outside there were entrances to shops. The main entrance, on St. Louis Street, led into the exchange, a domed rotunda said to be the most beautiful in America. Here, every day between noon and three half a dozen auctions were always going on at once. The rotunda was surrounded with arcades and galleries where women and children sauntered and men transacted business. In 1842, George Buckingham reported that when he walked through the rotunda, each auctioneer was

endeavouring to drown every voice but his own . . . One was selling pictures, and dwelling on their merits; another was disposing of ground-lots in embryo cities . . . and another was disposing of some slaves. These consisted of an unhappy negro family, who were all exposed to the hammer at the same time. Their good qualities were enumerated in English and in French, and their persons were carefully examined by intending purchasers, among whom they were ulti-

---

Top right. The St. Louis Hotel in its heyday before the Civil War.

Right. Auctions in the rotunda, St. Louis Hotel. Harriet Beecher Stowe imagined the sale of Uncle Tom and his fellow slaves from the St. Clare plantation as taking place in a New Orleans hotel rotunda.

mately disposed of, chiefly to Creole buyers; the husband at 750 dollars, the wife at 550, and the children at 220 each.

To reach the main part of the hotel, patrons used an entrance on Royal Street, and climbed a staircase leading to the public rooms and dining rooms. The bedrooms, which could accommodate up to 600 guests, occupied the two top floors. There was also a bar that one British visitor described as "not quite as large as the reading-room of the British Museum" and a ballroom whose painted ceiling by Domenico Canova was, according to Norman, "of beauty unsurpassed in America."

Before the Civil War, the St. Louis Hotel was the elegant center of Creole society. Creole gentlemen drank in the bar and brought their wives and daughters to concerts and *bals de societé*. During the winter of 1842–43, the ballroom was the scene of the most glittering party New Orleans had seen: a ball in honor of Henry Clay, who was paying the city an official visit. Subscriptions were $100 each. Six hundred guests sat down for dinner, during which music was provided by the orchestra of the French opera.

During the Reconstruction period, the St. Louis was used for a few years by the state legislature. Then the entire hotel, which had become very run-down, was renovated and provided with cast-iron verandahs. The name was changed to the Royal. Despite these efforts, it never recovered its former cachet. The French Quarter was by now shabby, and out-of-town visitors preferred the ambiance of the St. Charles.

The architect J. N. B. de Pouilly had laid out a pedestrian alley, Exchange Passage, which ran between Exchange Place at Iberville Street to opposite the entrance of the St. Louis Hotel on St. Louis Street. He intended all the buildings on this passage to have facades to harmonize with the hotel. The project was not completed, but a few of de Pouilly's buildings may still be seen in what remains of Exchange Passage. The block facing the hotel was leveled in 1905 to make way for the large building now occupied by the Wildlife and Fisheries Department. This wholesale destruction represented an earnest attempt to improve the neighborhood. It was the view of most New Orleans city planners in those days that all the old buildings in the French Quarter ought to be razed.

In 1912, John Galsworthy visited New Orleans and wrote what might be called a kind of epitaph for the St. Louis. The old place was then empty, visited only by tourists who were inveigled by itinerant guides into viewing the rotunda and the slave block. An old woman escorted

Galsworthy and his party into the gloomy, damp rotunda. As they picked their way through the corridors,

there came to us wandering — strangest thing that ever strayed through deserted grandeur — a brown, broken horse, lean, with a sore flank and a head of tremendous age. It stopped and gazed at us, as though we might be going to give it things to eat, then passed on, stumbling over the ruined marbles.

They went on into the rotunda, and the old woman lighted newspapers and held them up to show the slave block.

For a moment the whole shadowy room seemed full of forms and faces . . . "Yes, suh. Here they all came — 'twas the finest hotel — before the war-time; old Southern families — buyin' an' sellin' their property . . . And here were the bells to all the rooms. Broken, you see — all broken!"

Left. This photograph was taken during the demolition of the St. Louis Hotel in 1915, and shows the clay pots, lying on their sides in a honeycomb pattern, that the architects used to lighten the weight of the dome. Note the poster advertising *The Birth of a Nation*.

Right. The grand staircase, St. Louis Hotel.

In 1915, a bubonic plague scare in the city called attention to the fact that enormous numbers of rats were making their headquarters in the closed-up old hotel. It was, therefore, demolished. The Royal Orleans Hotel now occupies the site.

•

There were never any other hotels in New Orleans in a class with the St. Louis and the St. Charles. The nearest competitor was the Verandah, which flourished from 1838 to 1855 across the street from the St. Charles. The Verandah was named for its ironwork gallery, painted green, which circled the second story. This was the first iron gallery in New Orleans to project over the entire sidewalk, a style that was to become typical of the city. The hotel, designed by James and Charles Dakin in 1836, had other distinguished features: a dining room with sculpted chimneypieces and three elliptical domes; a marble Venus in the ladies' parlor; and frescoes, probably painted by Domenico Canova (who seems to have had no competitors). Oakey Hall wrote that the Verandah "prides itself on its

---

The Verandah Hotel (right) on St. Charles Street was one of the first buildings in New Orleans to make an extensive use of iron galleries. It burned in 1855. The Veranda Hotel (left), with even more ironwork, flourished briefly on Lafayette Square for a few years before the Civil War.

cosiness . . . And there is about it altogether a home look and a home feeling as pleasing as it is novel for New Orleans.'' The inevitable conflagration overtook the Verandah in July 1855. It was not rebuilt, but a hotel with nearly the same name (Veranda) and more galleries opened its doors in 1858 on Camp Street at Lafayette Square.

Since Reconstruction days, New Orleans has had a good choice of hotels. In the 1870s, prices ranged from $4 a day at the St. Charles and the St. Louis down to $2 at the antiquated Orleans on Chartres Street. The City Hotel, at Camp and Common streets, then newly remodeled, charged from $3 to $4. Four substantial meals were included in the prices. A guidebook noted, ''No fee to waiter or servants is necessary.''

Built before the Civil War as Bishop's Hotel, this building was given a thorough renovation and a new name, the City Hotel, in about 1870. It stood at the corner of Camp and Common streets.

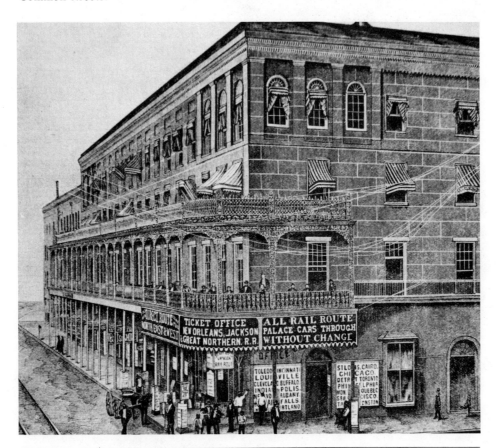

The Grunewald Hotel on University Place was enlarged in 1908 by adding a taller and more spacious annex on the site of the historic Mechanics' Institute. Now part of the Fairmont Hotel, the Grunewald is remembered by old-timers for the extraordinary decor of its restaurant, called The Cave. Inspired by the Mammoth Cave in Kentucky, The Cave occupied the basement of the Grunewald. Pipes, conduits, and beams were disguised as stalactites and stalagmites by the judicious application of 700,000 pounds of cement and plaster, and here and there among them sat naked stucco ladies. The Cave was a popular nightspot from about 1910 to 1930. Today, the cave effects and the maidens are gone and the room is used for a laundry.

Always a city of many transients and sightseers, New Orleans became expert at welcoming them: Now, over a million tourists a year are accommodated in dozens of comfortable hotels. But the St. Charles, in its various incarnations, and the St. Louis were more than that. They stood high among the great hotels of the world, and, as such, were too easily discarded.

The first Hotel Grunewald (left), seen here in 1895, was supplemented by a large and elaborate annex in 1908. In the basement of the newer building, which still stands, was the extraordinary restaurant known as The Cave (above). Here, one of its several life-size stucco nymphs modestly turns her back on the dining tables.

5

Health and Hazards

THE FIGHT AGAINST DISASTERS

During the great yellow fever epidemic of 1853, the New Orleans *Courier* assured its readers that they would not become ill if they remained calm. "Above all, keep your imagination from being frightened." Until well into this century, a torpid imagination was helpful to New Orleanians, beset by more than their share of frightening possibilities. Epidemics, hurricanes, and floods recurred again and again; devastating fires and death or serious illness from diseases resulting from poor sanitation were everyday occurrences. For many years, New Orleans had the highest death rate in the country. Even as late as 1880, when conditions had begun to improve, the death rate was 29.11 per 1000, compared to New York's 27.76, Chicago's 21.83, and St. Louis' 20.56.

The crime rate was (and still is) also high. And this fact probably explains why, in 1955, the police were sent for as a matter of course when bulldozers excavating for a new hotel in the French Quarter turned up human bones and skulls. It was not a case for the police, however, but for historians, who knew that the site had been used as a cemetery since

Left. The Girod Street Cemetery was the oldest Protestant burial ground in the city, filled with the graves of distinguished early citizens. The cemetery was obliterated in 1957.

at least 1724 and until the great fire of 1788, when it had been abandoned. No grave markers were found, for in that era the graves of ordinary citizens were either not marked at all or were marked with wooden crosses, which did not last long. In eighteenth-century New Orleans, the water table in the cemetery was less than two feet below the surface and stone markers would have sunk without a trace. However, in both France and Spain as well as in their colonies, only the rich expected a snug burial, perhaps inside a church or chapel. The corpses of ordinary people were wrapped in shrouds and laid into the earth — sometimes in a wooden coffin, but more often not. Bodies and coffins soon disintegrated and the burial site was used again.

The Americans, accustomed to six-foot-deep graves beneath solid granite headstones, were appalled by local burial customs. "Not a single grave stone marked the remains of either the noble or ignoble dead . . ." reported the New York merchant John Pintard in 1801. "Everyone who dies here must literally find a watery grave." And he added, ". . . a body is speedily devoured & transmigrated in crayfish or catfish — dressed by a French cook & feasted upon by a greasy Monk — a fair lady — a petit maître or a savage who in their turn supply some future banquet . . . Give my bones terra firma I pray — ."

The Creoles, for their part, were used to the traditional procedure, but lately they had been influenced by the revival in Europe of classic architecture and customs, a revival that included the Greek and Roman way of burying the dead in sarcophagi. Thus Creoles and Americans agreed that a tomb standing on the surface of the ground was a more acceptable burial place than a grave in New Orleans' watery and miasmic soil. If marble and granite were too heavy and expensive, brick and plaster were readily available and became the common materials for New Orleans tombs.

There was still the problem of space. Land was far too scarce and valuable for each deceased citizen to have his own tomb. The answer was to use the same tomb over and over again. In St. Louis Number One, which is the oldest New Orleans cemetery still in use, there are family tombs with space for only one or two bodies at a time that have accommodated ten generations of one family — as many as forty or fifty people. When each body disintegrated, as was bound to occur within a year, the remains were pushed to the back or deposited in a special lower vault, where they mingled with the dust and bones of earlier burials. The system is still followed.

Oven vaults, single vaults arranged three or four high and a score or more horizontally, were used for those who did not have access to a family tomb. New Orleans also had many society tombs — that is, tombs paid for by subscription by members of a society, giving them the privilege of being buried therein. The societies might be made up of people who followed the same trade or profession, or they might be purely social clubs. For example, the New Orleans Typographical Union and the Red River Pilots Association had their own tombs, while larger organizations such as the Odd Fellows and the firemen even had their own cemeteries. Or the societies might be for nothing more than burial insurance. Black people, not being allowed to join unions or white societies, were happy to subscribe for a few cents weekly to a burial association that guaranteed them a proper funeral and a decent final resting place.

The early cemeteries — St. Louis Number One and Number Two,

Left. Until only a few years ago, a vandalized burial vault was no uncommon sight in the older cemeteries. In 1913, Robert Haven Schauffer, a visitor to St. Louis Cemetery Number One, saw ''a score of individual graves, gaping wide open and with their inmates' bones exposed to view . . .'' He overhead a boy remark, ''Must be most a dollah's wuth o' bones in yare.''

Right. A view of tombs in the Girod Street Cemetery before most of the ironwork was stolen or destroyed.

Left. Oven tombs at St. Louis Cemetery Number One.

Bottom left. The "society tomb" of the New Orleans Battalion of Artillery in St. Louis Cemetery Number One. The design is by J. N. P. de Pouilly. There are sixteen niches, but many times that number of bodies have been entombed here. Each niche was used again and again.

Bottom right. A vandalized cast-iron gate at St. Patrick Cemetery Number Two.

Girod Street, and Lafayette Number One and Number Two — were quickly surrounded by the growing city. Today they are strange oases. One walks from a street teeming with life into a silent town of the dead. Decay is everywhere: leaning, sinking tombs, broken statuary and iron-work, and luxuriant crops of weeds that grow in cracks and crevices and on the roofs of vaults. Determined civic effort in recent years has checked some of this moldering, but has not erased it. The reason for the sad state of these old cemeteries is that their plots and tombs were originally sold with the understanding that the owners would keep them up. There was no such thing as perpetual care provided by the management of the cemetery. When relatives of the deceased died, moved away, or lost either their interest or their fortunes, the tombs became neglected. Lafcadio Hearn, writing over a hundred years ago during the yellow fever epidemic of 1878, described the situation, and, in some respects, he could have been writing today:

It is rather ghastly to have death in the midst of life as we have it in New Orleans . . . They are hideous Golgothas, these old intramural cemeteries of ours. In other cities the cemeteries are beautiful with all that the art of the gardeners and the sculptor can give. There horror is masked and hidden. Here it glares at us with empty sockets.

Furthermore, if we are to believe the testimony of earlier writers, New Orleans cemeteries have never been known for their orderliness or sanitation. In the 1820s an English visitor wrote, "In the Catholic burial-ground, which is in a swampy enclosure . . . the ground is so low, and overburied, that many discoloured bones, in monitory ghastliness, lie strewn about the turf; and I saw a slave digging a grave, which kept half filling itself with offensive water." In 1820, Benjamin Latrobe described a slave burial taking place in eighteen inches of water. The coffin "swam like a boat in the water," while children played with the bones and skulls that piled up as earth was dug for the grave.

During the city's ante-bellum heyday of wealth and lavish spending, the old cemeteries became filled with charming, beautiful, or perhaps merely curious cemetery art. Now, much of it has either crumbled or has been vandalized. Saddest of all was the Girod Street Cemetery. It became a refuge for winos and vagrants, who broke open tombs and crawled inside them at night for shelter. Girod Street was the final resting-place of many prominent citizens of New Orleans, but their bones received no more consideration than did those the children played with beside the anonymous slave's grave. In 1957, Christ Church Cathedral, owner of the cemetery, decided to put an end to its melancholy condition. The entire cemetery was deconsecrated and obliterated, and all the remains were taken away to mausoleums. An organization called Save Our Cemeteries came into being in the 1970s, too late to save Girod Street. Against considerable odds, this group is making good progress in preserving and restoring other threatened cemeteries.

·

In ante-bellum days, terrible epidemics decimated New Orleans every few years. At such times, graves and tombs could not be prepared fast enough. During the yellow fever epidemic of 1853 (to give just one example), interments at St. Patrick's Cemetery alone came to 1100 in one month.

At St. Patrick's, the dead were mostly poor immigrants newly arrived from Ireland. Immigrants, fresh from the ship, were always hard hit in epidemics, for not only did they live in slums, under poor sanitary conditions, but they were unaccustomed to hot, humid weather. Moreover, they were likely to be weakened by a grueling voyage in steerage. And, if the men found laboring jobs in construction or digging canals, they had to work in clouds of mosquitoes, the potential carriers of yellow fever and malaria. All the poor were in close contact with the contaminated water of the city's canals and gutters, which afforded cholera its means of spreading.

None of these sources were known then, of course. But since epidemics always struck in the hot season, some element in the climate, the terrain, or both was suspected.

"New Orleans has been built upon a site that only the madness of commercial lust could ever have tempted men to occupy," was the opinion, in 1853, of the *Illustrated London News* in an editorial about that summer's yellow fever epidemic in which 12,000 had died. New Orleanians did not care to hear such pronouncements. Yet any head of a household who could afford it sent his family out of town from May to October and went along himself if he could leave his business. The middle classes went to the Gulf Coast or to the farther shores of Lake Pontchartrain. The rich went north to White Sulphur Springs or any of several other spas, or even as far as Newport. People spoke of the Go-aways and the Can't-get-aways.

When an epidemic was in the offing, business suffered, and the Can't-get-aways believed that the least said about it the better. In 1810, the city council passed an ordinance forbidding the ringing of funeral bells between July 1 and December 31 of each year. Recurrent tolling, day and night, could be depressing, both to nerves and to commerce. "It is a standing maxim in the commercial world that nothing must be said that might injure trade," commented *DeBow's Magazine* in the 1850s. "Hence it is that the yellow fever has often prevailed in New Orleans to an alarming extent, before the journals were willing to admit that there was any cause for alarm." In early July 1853, when fifty-nine deaths from yellow fever clearly indicated that an epidemic was on the way, the newspapers devoted their headlines to a steam balloon ascension. Two weeks later, with the death rate soaring, the *Crescent* cautiously mentioned that the weather had been unusually rainy and cool, which might portend "a sickly season."

But the less-forthright *Orleanian* insisted, "We know of no prevalent diseases, nor do epidemics exist among us. The deaths are fewer in number than in any other city of similar population in the Union . . ." The same newspaper went on to say that those who got yellow fever were "poor — reckless and indifferent . . . less cautious and careful of themselves than are those habituated to our summers." Very likely, also, they drank "poisonously adulterated liquors." That week the deaths from yellow fever mounted to 204.

At the end of July, when corpses were piling up unburied because even a wage of $5 an hour could not attract enough gravediggers, the *Courier* and other papers reiterated the advice about not becoming frightened — to which *DeBow's* replied that if it was fright that killed, how did it happen that yellow fever swept off infants in vast numbers, "too young to know what fear is?"

The treatment one might get from a doctor varied according to what theory he followed. Some doctors advocated "heroic" treatment: doses of mercury to the point of salivation (the fatal dose) and massive bloodletting. George Buckingham, an English traveler who was taken ill while staying at the St. Charles in 1842, later wrote that twenty ounces of his blood were drawn by lancet and twenty more by eighty leeches applied to his throat. He praised the doctor, and said that he would never have survived without him. Other doctors believed that early diagnosis, bed rest, and a light diet was the only sensible treatment.

When an epidemic was unmistakably underway, the Common Council was called into emergency meeting (for those members who had not fled the city). After listening to speeches, they usually ended by ordering cannons to be fired all day long and pots of tar to be burned in the streets — two time-honored preventatives, both useless. Fortunately for New Orleans, there were several volunteer citizens' organizations who tended the sick. Of these the most notable was the Young Men's Howard Association, named for the eighteenth-century English reformer John Howard. The society was made up of clerks and other ordinary citizens who visited as many as seventy-five patients daily, dispensing simple advice, food, and medicine. They summoned doctors, found nurses, and, if necessary, helped with funeral arrangements and found shelter for widows and orphans. Supported by private donations and by modest handouts from the city, the Howard Association was founded in New Orleans in response to the cholera and yellow fever epidemic of 1832. This was years before the world had heard of Florence Nightingale or the Red Cross.

Since the causes of yellow fever and cholera were not known, it took courage to go into pestilence-infested houses; but remarkably few Howard Association members died as a result of doing so, perhaps because they were usually acclimatized — they had probably had light cases and had become immune. "The chance for an unacclimated young man from the North surviving the first summer, is by some considered as one to two," wrote Timothy Flint, one who did survive, in the 1820s. "The Americans come hither from all the states. Their object is to accumulate wealth and spend it somewhere else. But death — which they are very little disposed to take into the account — often brings them up before their scheme is accomplished."

As a last resort, desperately ill people were taken to a hospital or infirmary. New Orleans was rather better equipped with these institutions than many cities, but no hospital in the world at that time could have coped adequately with a big epidemic. The first Charity Hospital in New Orleans was built on Rampart Street in 1739 with money bequeathed to the city by a dying sailor. It was a rather rickety wooden building that

Left. New Orleans had an unusual number of private hospitals owned and operated by doctors. The medical profession was allowed to advertise.

Right. During epidemics, newspapers printed helpful tips such as this one.

went down in a hurricane in 1779. A second hospital on the same site burned in 1810. Henry Latrobe designed a third one, which was built in 1815 on Canal Street, between Baronne Street and University Place. It was described as plain but imposing, surrounded by a large garden. During the 1830s, the architect William Nichols converted it into the Louisiana State House. It was demolished about 1850, after the state government had moved to Baton Rouge.

In 1834, a fourth Charity Hospital was built on present-day Tulane Avenue. It was a simple, imposing edifice, three stories high, able to accommodate 500 patients. Sisters of Charity, paid by the state, were in charge of the nursing. An outbuilding housed the insane, although there were always more cases than could be taken care of and the Parish Prison also had a section for mental cases. Until late in the nineteenth century the treatment of the insane was appalling almost everywhere in the world and New Orleans was no exception. But, in general, Charity Hospital had an excellent reputation. The fourth building lasted just over a hundred years. It was razed in 1938 to make way for the present skyscraper hospital.

When it opened in 1834, Charity Hospital was the largest building in New Orleans. ''Here, the only passport required for admission to the best attendance is sickness or an injury,'' wrote Benjamin Norman, in his *New Orleans and Environs* (1845). ''No cold formalities are thrown in the way of the suffering patient. Indeed, it has become a subject of complaint, that access is so easy, and the position so agreeable, that the improvident and the indolent take undue advantage of its benefits.''

Other hospitals were owned and operated privately by doctors. There was the Franklin Infirmary, near the Pontchartrain railroad station, built in 1842 to care for 100 patients; Dr. Stone's Infirmary, under the aegis of New Orleans' most prestigious physician; the Hotel Dieu; and the Touro Infirmary, one of Judah Touro's philanthropies, occupying a once-grand Georgian mansion near the river.

Across the river at McDonoghville was the Marine Hospital, an impressive Gothic Revival building with crenelated towers and a parapet. It was constructed in 1838 after designs by Robert Mills, architect of the United States Treasury in Washington, D.C., and was built and operated by the federal government. On January 10, 1861, in one of the many incidents that led up to the Civil War, state troops seized the hospital, along with two forts and other government installations downriver from New Orleans. After war was declared, the Confederates transferred all the patients elsewhere and used the building as a powder magazine. On December 28, 1861, whether by accident or by arson, it blew up, shaking the city and the countryside for miles around.

The Civil War was another disaster for this city that knew disaster so

The oldest continuously operated private hospital in New Orleans is the Hotel Dieu. This was its first building, erected in 1858 and torn down not long after this picture was taken in 1910.

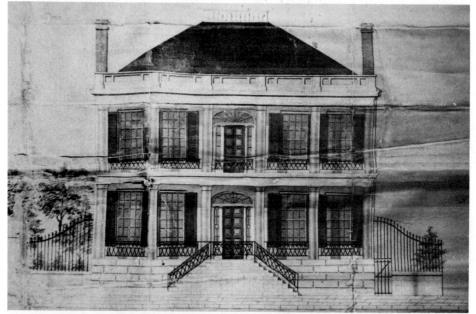

Left, top and middle. Touro Infirmary, still an important hospital, used to be on New Levee Street in a handsome building that had once been a private residence.

Bottom left. Marine Hospital was built in 1838 by the federal government, and the complaints about it sound very modern: it cost too much (over $1 million) and, in spite of that, it was poorly constructed, the basement being below flood level and too damp to use.

Below. The commanding general of the Union occupation forces, Benjamin Butler, enforced needed sanitation measures. Nevertheless, he was a man everybody loved to hate. Because the women of New Orleans made a point of being rude to Union men, even spitting on them, "Beast Butler" ordered that any woman who offended in this way should be subject to the same legal procedures as a common prostitute. The cartoon is a British reaction to his order.

well. The devastation was not physical; throughout the war, New Orleans looked much as it always had, and, if anything, better, because the commanding general, Benjamin F. Butler, insisted on cleaning up the streets and enforcing sanitation laws. Ben Butler was accused of helping himself to table silver (Silver Spoon Butler was one of his several uncomplimentary nicknames in New Orleans), but perhaps the most lastingly offensive thing he did was to lay railroad tracks along St. Joseph Street in Faubourg St. Mary, lowering the tone of that neighborhood for good. New Orleans was not burned, like Atlanta, and no battle took place there; the real devastation was to trade, which was completely ruined. As for the less-measurable realm of heart, spirit, and intellect, that was worst of all. The bitterness of occupation and Reconstruction was felt in this proud city for generations.

·

A city known as the necropolis of the south needed asylums for widows and orphans, and in an era with little respect for philanthropy, it did well. George Buckingham noted, "after all that I had heard of New Orleans and its dissipation and profligacy I had hardly expected to have found so many [charitable institutions] and so well supported." One of the first was the Asylum for Destitute Orphan Boys, established in the early 1820s by Nicholas Girod in an old plantation house. The Poydras Home, founded even earlier, was for girls. In the 1850s, soon after the great cholera epidemic, it acquired a "large and beautiful building and a model of an asylum" (according to a contemporary newspaper account). This was on Magazine Street, and so was the St. Elizabeth Asylum, built in 1856 and described as "massive enough to stand through all time." (Perhaps so, but within fifteen years it burned to the ground.) Most orphanages were financed and run by one of the major religious groups. The relatively small Jewish community built the Jewish Widows and Orphans Home on

Right. The masses of orphans in New Orleans can be imagined from the large size of the orphanages. The Episcopal Children's Home (above) and the Jewish Widows and Orphans Home (below), both built in the 1880s, were usually filled to capacity.

Left. One of the oldest of the city's numerous orphanages was the Female Orphan Asylum at the intersection of Camp and Prytania streets. It was built in 1840, a plain, well-proportioned brick building with a Greek Revival doorway. When this photograph was taken, it had acquired galleries and Second Empire embellishments. The orphanage, which housed 160 little girls, is gone now, but the statue in front of it is not. It represents Margaret Haughery, a poor Irish immigrant who made enough money in a bakery business to care for countless orphans. This homage to Margaret (as everyone called her) was the first such public tribute to a woman in the United States. The little park in which it stands is called Margaret Place.

Left, middle and bottom. New Orleans was a precarious place for old people without means. Judah Touro, the Jewish philanthropist, left money for an interdenominational alms house. It burned during the Civil War, while Union troops were quartered in it. Another was built on Danneel Street in the 1880s and named for Judah Touro and Mayor Joseph A. Shakspeare.

Jackson Avenue just before the war. In the 1880s, they built another such home on St. Charles Avenue. Thomy Lafon, one of the city's few millionaires "of color," left large sums of money for black and white orphans and widows. And there were other such charitable efforts, but in this city where catastrophe was commonplace, never enough.

Disease was the greatest maker of widows and orphans. Infants died in large numbers of cholera infantum, which was not cholera at all, but a kind of dysentery with similar symptoms. Infant mortality in New Orleans was double or even triple that of other eastern cities (and it was high everywhere). There were also countless unidentified fevers, aches, and pains that killed or debilitated. The English-born architect Thomas Wharton, who moved to New Orleans from Connecticut during the 1850s and died there in 1862, suffered most of the time from "bilious neuralgia" and "excess of bile," for which he consulted Dr. Stone, "the highest authority."

Mysterious illnesses had plagued the citizenry since colonial times. In about 1800, the French traveler C. C. Robin wrote that he was sure the cause of unhealthfulness in New Orleans was the too great congestion of houses: "When New Orleans was first laid out its little wooden houses were well spaced and did not confine the air or reflect the sun's rays as the present, large, closely-built edifices coated with lime must do." He also deplored the cutting of swamp trees, which, he pointed out, provided healthful shade and coolness. Other commentators on health conditions didn't think much of the trees: the author of an account of the 1853 epidemic wrote, "From the rear of the city to Lake Pontchartrain, from four to five miles, is a pestiferous swamp, filled with funereal-looking cypress trees, and generally covered with water."

But if the cause of yellow fever was not tall houses, or trees, or the lack of them, what could it be? One doctor announced that it was a "wingless animalcula," a kind of germ that got about in hot weather. Others believed the cause to be intemperance, or irreligion, or taking too much castor oil, or the presence in New Orleans of too many different races and nationalities. (The Know-Nothing Party of the 1850s, the political party that wanted to keep America Anglo-Saxon and Protestant, had a large following in New Orleans, including — curiously enough — many French-Spanish Roman Catholics.) Two leading New Orleans physicians, doctors McFarlane and Cartwright, announced after the 1853 epidemic that yellow fever could be cured by *spreading* filth. They believed that filth would kill the "causative agent," whatever it was, and they insisted that their studies had shown that "areas of greatest filth had relatively low yellow fever rates." Cartwright added that "terrene poison" was the cause, a lethal agent presumably brought up from the earth by canal digging.

For a century or more, there was a running battle between those who were sure the two big pestilences were brought by ships and who wanted to institute a quarantine the minute any cases were reported, and those who thought quarantine a foolish waste of time and a handicap to business. The result of quarantine, when instituted, was certainly a cleaner, less congested port, which probably reduced the incidence of illness. During the Civil War, the Confederates hoped that an epidemic would wipe out Union troops occupying New Orleans, but, at least partly because of General Butler's strict laws regarding sanitation as well as a rigid quarantine, no epidemic occurred. There was a light epidemic in 1866, after the Union Army and its regulations had departed, and a serious one in 1867.

Despite the Board of Health, most of the streets continued to be filthy until the beginning of this century. This was partly because the health officials were political appointees who knew nothing about health; and partly because most streets were unpaved and the water system rudimentary. Floods and crevasses were also a constant dread, and when they occurred business came to a standstill. Water was a ruling factor in New Orleans life: too little pure water, too much dirty water. The writer Rebecca Harding Davis, visiting the city in the 1880s, noted that the water, a deadly enemy here, perpetually fought and forced back, rushes in, whenever a day's rain gives it vantage, at every crevice; floods the streets and clogs the drains. It oozes out of the ground wherever you step on it, drips down the walls of your drawing-room, stains your books a coffee-color, clings to you, chilly and damp, in your clothes and in your bed, turns the air you breathe into a cold steam, and washes your dead out of their graves.

Mrs. Davis' mention of drawing rooms and books shows that she was writing of the well-to-do classes; and George Washington Cable, writing of New Orleans floods at about the same time, emphasized that the business district and the wealthier suburbs, being on higher ground, were usually not flooded.

The merchant goes and comes between his home and his counting-room as usual in the tinkling street-cars, merely catching glimpses of the water down the cross streets. The humbler classes, on the other hand, suffer severely . . . Skiffs enter the poor man's parlor and bedroom to bring the morning's milk or to carry away to higher ground his goods and chattels . . . the house-cat sits on the gatepost; huge rats come swimming, in mute and loathsome despair, from that house to this one, and are pelted to death from the windows. Even snakes seek the same asylum.

To build an efficient drainage and sewerage system for New Orleans was possibly the most difficult engineering problem in the whole world. Until as late as 1897, the drainage system was almost medieval. Rain from heavy rainstorms ran through deep open gutters into open canals back of town, which emptied into the swamp or Lake Pontchartrain. The water was helped on its way by engine-driven paddle wheels, but these were almost useless when the canals became clogged with vegetation and raw sewage (which left the city by the same route). A severe storm could flood parts of the city for days.

It was clear that while this state of affairs lasted, New Orleans would never be a modern city and, finally, in 1895, a commission was established to attack the problem. The old idea that the terrain of New Orleans was a swamp "that no human power can drain, and no effort can penetrate" was still generally believed, but engineers agreed that it was not true. It could be done. All that was needed was over a billion dollars plus about twenty years of work. It was a matter of building dozens of pumping stations that would lift the water in several stages from the trough of the swamp over the levee into Lake Pontchartrain or Lake Borgne; of cleaning and covering the existing canals and of digging 95 miles of new ones; and of building thousands of miles of pipelines and subsurface drain lines as well as a gigantic power plant to provide electricity for the pumps. By 1914, such a system was completed and in operation; but draining New Orleans turned out to be an ongoing challenge. As soon as the established sections of town became more livable, a new population flocked in and at once there were new built-up areas to be drained. The great swamp back of town is dry now, but other soggy areas of the outskirts of the city are being subdivided and built upon.

As for drinking water, wells in the city were contaminated before the end of the Spanish era, and one of the first concerns of the Americans was to construct a waterworks. The first one, designed by Benjamin Latrobe, was soon inadequate for the rapidly growing city. The water, of course, was of dubious purity and carried so much sediment that it was dark brown in color, but none of this seemed to have troubled its consumers, for it had a mystic reputation for being pure, even curative.

A second waterworks, built in the 1830s, had iron pipes and functioned somewhat better than the first. Water was pumped from the river into a reservoir, allowed to settle, and then pumped to subscribers. Among the subscribers was the St. Charles Hotel. In a letter written in 1844 on the St. Charles letterhead, a young girl noted that "after it has been purified it is the most delightful water to drink I ever tasted. The purifying process is as follows. Thick dirty water is put into a large stone jar, a small piece of alum is thrown in, after an hour you may draw off a tumbler full as clear as a cristol and pure as spring water. The mud adheres to the sides and bottom of the jar."

Whatever the quality of the water, the rates of the waterworks company were high, and most homeowners preferred to collect rainwater in cisterns. Although rain was cleaner and more attractive in appearance than river water, the deadly aspect of cisterns went unrecognized: namely, that they provided splendid breeding places for mosquitoes, including *stegomyia aegypti*, the yellow fever carrier. This lethal insect also bred in the gutters, in the nearby swamps, in buckets of water that theaters were

---

Right. This meticulously accurate map of New Orleans was prepared in 1863 for the use of the Union Army. Besides roads and railway lines, canals, and fortifications, it shows the formidable swamps and forests still to be conquered by the spreading city.

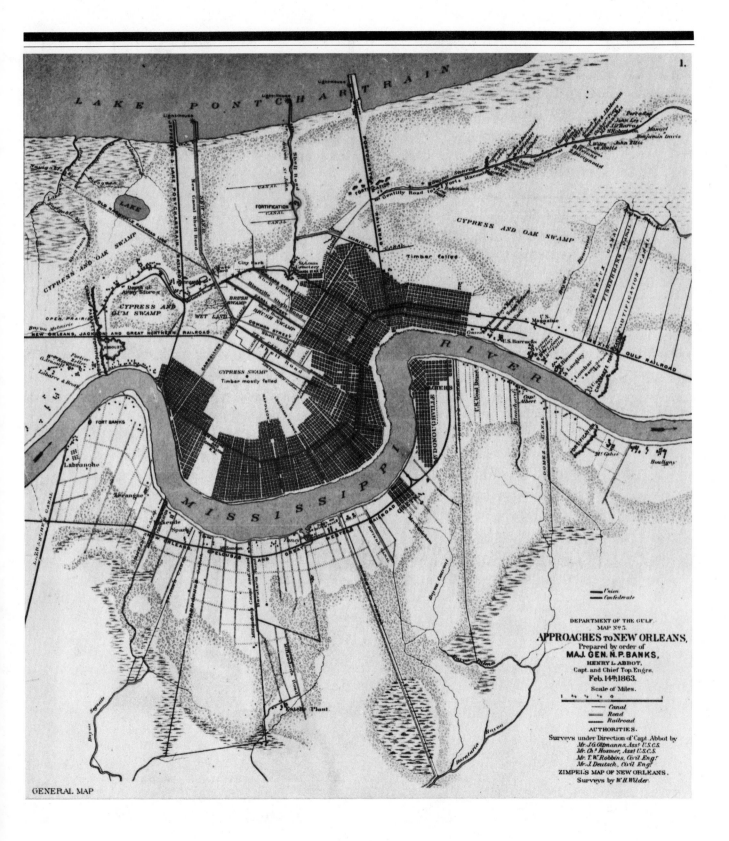

GENERAL MAP

required by law to keep ready in case of fire, and in vases of flowers left in front of tombs in the cemeteries.

Even though no one then knew that certain mosquitoes were killers, just the terrible biting they did was a distressing part of daily life in all seasons except the short winter. Harriet Martineau, who visited New Orleans in May 1849, wrote, "The moschetoes [sic] were a great and perpetual plague . . . Many ladies are accustomed, during the summer months, to get after breakfast into a large sack of muslin tied round the throat, with smaller sacks for the arms, and to sit thus at work or book, fanning themselves to protect their faces. I wore gloves and prunella boots all day long, but hands and feet were stung through all the defences I could devise." The children of the well-to-do played inside tents made of netting, while child slaves were set to work at an early age waving peacock feathers in the dining room or following Missus about the house with a fan. People even walked along the street with netting suspended from their hats or bonnets.

The last big yellow fever epidemic took place in 1878. As usual, there was an attempt to cover it up. The first death was that of a ship's purser from Brazil, who died in a New Orleans boarding house on May 29. More cases soon followed, but there was no official report of yellow fever cases until July 12. By the end of the summer, 4000 people had died in the city and many others in cities and towns on the Gulf and up the river. In New Orleans, 27,000 became ill but recovered — a sign that, at least, medical treatment had improved since former epidemics. Business losses were in the millions. That winter, a group of businessmen, tired of the city

In this drawing from the Notarial Archives, pipes carry rainwater from rooftop gutters into a cistern. Scarcely a house in New Orleans was without one.

council's apathy, organized the Auxiliary Sanitary Association to employ cleaners for streets and privies.

The idea that mosquitoes might have something to do with yellow fever was suggested in 1881 by Charles Finlay of Havana, but not proven until the famous experiments in Cuba in 1901. However, it took another outbreak of yellow fever, in 1905, to convince New Orleans. When twenty people died of the disease in the early summer of that year, the city authorities started after the mosquitoes, launching a campaign against stagnant water, and forcing citizens to cover and oil their cisterns. In 1918, cisterns were finally outlawed.

Cisterns had been New Orleans landmarks for about a hundred years — not landmarks that one can regret doing away with, since they were neither sanitary nor beautiful (although sometimes they were attractively decorated with ironwork), but a part of lost New Orleans that old-timers still speak of. Mark Twain, in *Life on the Mississippi,* called the cistern " a mighty cask, painted green, and sometimes a couple of stories high . . . But the people cannot have wells, and so they take rainwater. Neither can they conveniently have cellars or graves . . . so they do without both, and few of the living complain, and none of the others."

·

Fire was another great hazard. Terrible fires have always swept great cities, but New Orleans seemed particularly vulnerable. For one thing, its chief export, cotton, was highly inflammable, and mountains of it were always present in a relatively small dock and warehouse area. Until the late 1800s, most buildings were at least partly made of wood, and narrow streets, poor communication, and a lack of piped water made fire fighting difficult. In the early days, fire companies were elite groups of volunteers, rather like men's clubs. After 1855, firemen were salaried, but fire companies were likely to be made up of rowdies. In either category, there was always an irresponsible element that arrived drunk or did not arrive at all.

After 1803, the American authorities tried to organize better fire protection for a city that had nearly burned down twice within one generation. The Bucket Ordinance required every household to own at least two fire buckets. Theaters were ordered to dig two wells and keep casks and buckets of water on hand, along with axes, sledge hammers, gaffs, and hooks. Similar requirements were made for other public places. When, in 1839, the St. Charles Theater caught fire and was burning out of control,

James Dakin designed this little firehouse in 1841. It is shown here draped in purple and black for a funeral. The city acquired its first steam fire engine in 1855. It was pulled by four horses and needed a separate wagon to carry its fuel and hose. On the way to its first fire it plunged through a wooden bridge. But the city persevered and by 1860 had six more. By that time, also, a wireless alarm system had replaced the old method of ringing church bells to sound fire alarms.

firemen actually succeeded in extinguishing the flames. It was the first such instance on record in the city, and the amazed and grateful theater owner, James Caldwell, invited all the firemen to the next performance and made it a benefit on their behalf.

Despite precautions, ante-bellum New Orleans produced spectacular fires on the average of about one every ten days. Not only did important buildings burn down, such as the Orleans Cotton Press, and the St. Charles and St. Louis hotels, but so did countless warehouses and small houses. In 1848, five steamboats burned while tied up at the levee, and the flames spread into the city for several blocks.

"Apropos of fire," wrote George Rose, an English visitor in the 1880s, "it has struck me frequently and forcibly as a marvellous thing that all America is not burned to the ground, through the careless way in which lucifer matches are used. At every turn you find them lying about in most dangerous proximity to other combustible matter."

If, in New Orleans, catastrophe struck more spectacularly than elsewhere, on the other hand in no other American place was there so much gaiety, lavishness, and sheer dedication to good times. The city had a need to balance disaster with joy. Surely it was no accident that the ancient European custom of a pre-Lenten carnival should have been so enthusiastically embraced by New Orleans. And, since paradox is tantalizing and tension between opposites generates new vitality, these factors are clearly among the reasons for the city's ceaseless fascination.

J.R.Grabert

N.O.

Mind and Spirit

SCHOOLS, LIBRARIES, AND PLACES OF WORSHIP

"A library in Louisiana is as rare as a Phoenix," declared Berquin-Duvallon, a refugee from Santo Domingo, in 1802, "There are not ten men of polite literary attainments, whose minds have been embellished, who are capable of appreciating the merit of a Descartes and a Newton, a Mallebranche and a Locke, a Buffon and a Linnaeus . . . You, therefore, who delight in the belles-lettres, shun, I conjure you, the banks of the Mississippi. The very air of that region is mortal to the muse." As a displaced person, monsieur Berquin-Duvallon may have taken a jaundiced view, but it was one that others corroborated. The French traveler, C. C. Robin, describing New Orleans at about the same time, reported, "No one has thought of writing the names of the streets on each corner . . . even if there were signs only a very few could read them."

The Spanish regime had established an elementary school, whose

---

Left. President William Howard Taft's official visit to New Orleans in 1912 included a Sunday stop at the Unitarian Church at Peters Avenue (now Jefferson Avenue) and Danneel Street. The New Orleans sculptor Angela Gregory, then a small girl, remembers presenting the president with violets and also remembers her acute disappointment when he sat on them.

---

classes were conducted in Spanish or Latin. Since most of the population spoke French, the school was poorly attended. According to a governor's report of 1788, there were never more than thirty children in the school and sometimes as few as six. French-speaking parents preferred to send their children to small private schools, with classes conducted in their own language, or to have them tutored at home. When the Americans came they fell in with this custom. If an advanced education was wanted, they sent their sons north. Most girls, whether Creole or American, were not expected to learn much beyond the Three Rs and a few ladylike accomplishments, such as drawing, dancing, and embroidery plus etiquette and pleasing manners. Eliza Ripley, writing of her New Orleans childhood in the 1840s, recalled that she and her friends attended a private school run by a schoolmaster who, to punish them, forced them to kneel on tacks. When their parents found out, the little girls were kept home. For some of them it was probably the end of their education. Sometimes older girls were sent to be "finished" in New York or Baltimore.

In 1811, the state legislature appropriated $20,000 to establish the College of Orleans. Fees were charged to all except fifty charity scholars. The charity seats were never filled because of a social stigma attached to accepting handouts. As George Washington Cable wrote in 1885, looking back at those years, "The idea was still that of condescending benevolence, not of a paying investment by society for its own protection and elevation." The College of Orleans struggled to survive, but after about fifteen years it went out of existence.

During the boom years of the 1830s, when the population doubled and money was lavished on the building of houses, hotels, theaters, churches, and railroads, almost nothing was spent on either schools or libraries. There were several "reading rooms" in the commercial exchanges, but these did not include books. "Reading," for the city's businessmen, meant newspapers, periodicals, stock quotations, and ships' schedules. Perhaps, since illiteracy was the norm, there seemed little need for libraries. In 1846, two rooms of the Merchants' Exchange were set aside as a library, which was open to the public and contained 7500 books. In 1850, Abijah Fisk, a prominent businessman, gave a library to the city, but it was years before it found suitable quarters, in the Mechanics Institute. In 1850, there were 100 books to every 1218 free citizens; if slaves had been included, the proportion would have been 100 books to every 2310 persons. In Massachusetts, the same year, there were 100 books to every 206 persons.

Because of the frequent epidemics, medicine was much on the public mind. In 1843, seven doctors joined to found a medical school, for which James Dakin designed a charming Greek Revival building at Common Street and University Place. Two years later, Dakin added a similar building next door, to house a law school. These units formed the basis of a new institution, to be called the University of Louisiana.

What was most sorely needed in New Orleans was a public school system, and early in the 1850s help for such a project came from an unexpected quarter. One of New Orleans' many self-made men was John McDonogh, a Marylander who had arrived in the city shortly before the Stars and Stripes, and had made an enormous fortune. McDonogh was a reclusive old bachelor, regarded as a pinchpenny and an eccentric. People disliked him, because he was not gregarious and didn't drink in bars, or gamble, or go to balls. Even stranger, he offered his slaves a chance to buy their freedom and go to Liberia. Granted, it took them most of their working years to save the necessary money; but they had something to hope for and some of them actually realized that hope. McDonogh had a plantation on the west bank and when he traveled back and forth to the city he did so by rowboat. People said this was because he was too stingy to pay the ferry. Children used to tease him in the streets. But when he died, in 1850, and his will was read, it turned out that he had left more than two million dollars for the education of white children in New Orleans and Baltimore. Soon after the Civil War, when the city had no money at all for education, McDonogh funds built and operated thirty schools and more have been added since. There are still some of these sturdy, simple Victorian buildings in use, but most have been replaced by larger and more modern ones. McDonogh Schools remain a part of the childhood memories of many thousands of New Orleanians.

The public was abashed by its malicious treatment of old McDonogh. To make amends, the legislature had a bust of him made and set up in Lafayette Square. For years, schoolchildren brought bouquets of flowers there on McDonogh Day, the first Friday in May. The ceremony now takes place on Duncan Plaza, before a newer bust by the New Orleans sculptor, Angela Gregory.

In higher education, the city's most celebrated philanthropist was Paul Tulane. The son of a French Huguenot from Santo Domingo, Tulane was born in Princeton, New Jersey, in 1801. As a young man of twenty-two he went to New Orleans and became a merchant. By the time of the Civil War, he was one of New Orleans' legendary self-made successes and had

amassed a large fortune in real estate. Unlike many southern tycoons, he managed to hold on to his fortune in spite of the war. He spent his later years in the north, but he never forgot New Orleans and its need for a university. In his will he left all his New Orleans real estate fortune to the languishing little University of Louisiana. In 1884, the medical and law buildings on Common Street (present Tulane Avenue), which had been used during Reconstruction for classes for freedmen, became the nucleus of a greatly expanded institution, and the old name was changed to Tulane University. The present site on St. Charles Avenue was acquired in 1895, at which time the Common Street buildings were vacated and, later, demolished.

In 1887, Mrs. Josephine Louise Newcomb established a college for young women in memory of her daughter, Harriott Sophie Newcomb. The first classes were held in an Italianate house at Howard and Camp streets, then in a larger establishment on Camp Street, and later in the Robb house (see page 88). Besides offering a good academic course, Newcomb developed a superior pottery department, turning out art nouveau vases and decorative objects that are now collectors' items. And not only that: Newcomb was the first female institution in the south to put its young ladies into gym bloomers.

Among free persons of color there had always been some degree of education, obtained privately. The end of the Civil War found some of them very well educated, and the majority were not much worse off than the poorer classes of whites. But the freed slaves were nearly 100 percent illiterate. Northern religious groups and private individuals sent money to New Orleans to help with their education. The American Missionary Association started Southern University in New Orleans. It moved to Baton Rouge in 1913. Another institution especially for blacks was Union Normal School, later New Orleans University, which occupied its own five-story, turreted brick building on St. Charles Avenue. Another black

---

Top left. This building on Common Street, designed in the 1840s by James Dakin, housed the University of Louisiana when it was founded in 1847. After 1884, it became part of the newly established Tulane University. The site, which included other buildings, is now occupied by part of the Fairmont Hotel.

Bottom left. For many years, McDonogh elementary schools were a part of the average New Orleans childhood. This one was across the river, where the donor of the schools, John McDonogh, had lived.

school was Straight University, which began classes in 1870 in a building on Esplanade Avenue and later acquired its own new building at Canal and Tonti streets. Although these institutions were called universities, the curriculum began with the Three Rs, which was what most of the students needed, and progressed as far as they could afford to go. Even at fees of only a few dollars a month, few students could finance an extended education, and in any case there were not many opportunities waiting in the outside world for educated blacks. Nevertheless, these schools managed to survive until 1935, when they were incorporated into the new, larger, and academically superior Dillard University, and moved to the Dillard campus in Gentilly, on the other side of town. The Christian Brothers bought the old property on St. Charles Avenue, demolished the red brick building, and replaced it with a modern school, de la Salle Academy. The house formerly occupied by New Orleans University's president was a fine old raised villa, known as the Gould House. Preservationists raised funds to move it to Audubon Park, but in the end the Park Commission refused to accept it, and it was razed.

•

Despite the city's reputation for wickedness, New Orleans has not lacked for churches since its earliest days. The old church of St. Louis, originally built by the French, was destroyed in the fire of 1788. A new one was dedicated as a cathedral on December 24, 1794. In 1849, plans were made to restore it, but it had deteriorated so badly that it was torn down and replaced by the present cathedral. St. Patrick's Church, built in the 1830s by James Dakin, survives, as does the Ursuline convent, the only eighteenth-century French building left in the city. The second Ursuline convent and chapel, built in the 1820s and for nearly a hundred years a riverfront landmark, was demolished in 1912. In its place is the Industrial Canal, the construction of which added eleven miles to the dock area. On the grounds of the convent were two old plantation houses, one used as

Top left. Tulane Medical School was designed by Thomas Sully in 1893. It occupied the entire block on Canal Street between Robertson and Villere streets.

Bottom left. Sophie Newcomb College started off in 1887 in the Hale mansion on the corner of Camp and Delord streets (now Howard Avenue). At that time, this was a neighborhood of substantial Italianate mansions. Almost none of them is still standing.

The Ursuline Sisters' second convent was begun in 1823, the chapel in 1829. The third story and the clock were added in the 1850s. For years, the big rococo clock was a landmark, visible from steamboats up and down the river. In 1912, the buildings were destroyed to make way for the Industrial Canal.

an orphanage and the other as a residence for priests. These were razed as well. Another landmark Catholic church was St. Katherine's on Tulane Avenue, a fine example of Gothic Revival. After the Reconstruction period, its congregation became exclusively black.

In ante-bellum days, Catholic churches had not been segregated, and other denominations had provided a special gallery for the use of slaves and people of color. With the hardening of racial prejudice at the turn of the century, black people ceased to attend white churches and had their own instead.

The Methodists had been the first to have a church especially for blacks, the Wesleyan Chapel, built on St. Paul Street near Poydras, in 1844. Its slave congregation made the bricks for it and were also the construction workers. In 1859, blacks were forbidden to hold church services, at the Wesleyan Chapel or anywhere else. After the war the Methodists were strong among black churchgoers in New Orleans. Baptists were even stronger. The now-demolished Pilgrim Rest Baptist Church on Louisiana Avenue was one of several that, for years, had a white pastor and a black congregation, a system that no longer exists.

The First Methodist Episcopal Church at Poydras and Carondelet streets was designed by Dakin and Dakin in 1836. A mixture of Egyptian and Greek styles, it was described by a contemporary guidebook as possessing a "novel grandeur and beauty to be seen in no other similar structure in the Union." It was built at the same time as the St. Charles Hotel and burned at the same time as well, in 1851, when the fire raging at the St. Charles sent a shower of hot sparks to its roof.

Since the 1880s, Episcopalians have had their Christ Church Cathedral on St. Charles Avenue, but three earlier Christ Churches are no more. The first was an octagonal brick building on Canal Street, designed by Henry Latrobe. No picture of it exists. It was replaced in 1835–37 by a low-domed, Greek Revival building of considerable distinction, designed by Gallier and Dakin. About ten years later, the parish exchanged it for land owned by Judah Touro further out on Canal Street at the corner of Dauphine, where they built a third church, designed by Thomas Wharton. Touro took over the second Christ Church and converted it into a synagogue. This he presented to the Spanish-Portuguese Jewish congregation of New Orleans, which until then had been meeting in rented rooms. Old Mr. Touro moved into the former rectory next door to the synagogue, and died there in 1854. Both the synagogue and the Touro residence were torn down to make room for the Touro Row commercial buildings.

Top left. This classic Greek Revival building was designed in 1835 by Gallier and Dakin for the congregation of Christ Episcopal Church. It was the second church of that name to occupy the corner of Canal and Bourbon streets. By 1846, the neighborhood was becoming commercial, and, according to Creole custom, shops were open on Sunday. A new Christ Church was erected on a quieter corner down the street, and the old one became a synagogue.

Top right. The third Christ Church at Canal and Dauphine streets was designed by Thomas Wharton and its construction supervised by James Gallier, in 1846. When, forty years later, the congregation elected to build the present Christ Church Cathedral on St. Charles Avenue, this church was sold and demolished to make way for the Mercier Building.

Bottom left and right. Temple Sinai on Carondelet Street at Calliope was completed in 1872. For one hundred and six years it was one of the landmarks of the city. After its congregation moved to a new temple on St. Charles Avenue in 1928, the building was used for offices, and, later, for a theater. It is shown at right during demolition in 1977.

In the 1870s, Temple Sinai was built on Carondelet Street, between Delord and Calliope streets, described in an 1885 guide as "the most beautiful edifice of its kind in the United States." Its two lofty golden turrets were prominent landmarks, visible from all over the city, until the building was demolished in 1977.

The First Presbyterian Church was designed by William Brand in 1819 and stood at St. Charles and Gravier streets. Its first minister died of yellow fever in 1820, and was succeeded by Theodore Clapp, summoned from New England. Some years after, Reverend Clapp astonished his parishioners by becoming a Unitarian. Instead of Clapp leaving, the congregation left, and built another church on Lafayette Square. Judah Touro, a friend of Reverend Clapp, bought the old church for him and Clapp continued to preach there until it was destroyed in the burning of the first St. Charles Hotel. Harriet Martineau, the English journalist and traveler, described the church when she attended its services one Sunday in 1849:

The structure had quite the appearance of a "Friends Meeting House." It was of unpainted brick, entirely devoid of any ornamentation. The little steeple was only high enough and big enough to hold a small bell. One entered a narrow vestibule, with two doors leading into the body of the church, and two flights of stairs to respective galleries. It was further furnished with two conspicuous tin signs: "Strangers Gallery on the Right" and "Gallery for Colored Persons on the Left."

The main floor of the church was reserved for the regular parishioners.

Left. The second St. Paul's Episcopal Church at Camp and Gaiennie streets was built in 1893 to replace an ante-bellum brick structure, which burned down in 1891. This one lasted until the late 1950s, when the Mississippi Bridge and its approaches wiped out nine blocks in this neighborhood.

Above. The modest brick structure that became known as Dr. Clapp's Church was one of the earliest Protestant places of worship in New Orleans. It was built in 1819 and burned in 1851, another victim of the fire at the nearby St. Charles Hotel.

The second Presbyterian Church, on Lafayette Square. This "large and elegant Gothic building, after the style of the fourteenth century, turreted all around" (as the *Delta* described it when it opened its doors in 1856) was designed by Henry Howard, replacing an earlier Greek Revival church, which had burned. The church was torn down in the 1930s.

In those days it was the custom in most protestant churches for each family to buy, or rent, a pew and keep it exclusively for their own use.

During the early nineteenth century, a substantial number of the new arrivals from the north were Presbyterians, and they built themselves a handsome Greek Revival church on Lafayette Square. "An edifice of the Grecian Doric order," said Norman's guidebook. " — the handsomest public place in the city. The basement story is of granite, but the rest of the construction is brick, plastered to imitate stone." The church had a domed interior, lighted by a handsome chandelier, and seated 1500 worshipers. It succumbed to one of New Orleans' countless fires and was replaced in 1856 by a fine Gothic building designed by Henry Howard. This church was an ornament to Lafayette Square until the 1930s, when it was replaced by a federal office building. The Third Presbyterian Church (later the Roman Catholic Church of the Holy Redeemer), on Washington Square, was a charming little brick structure with a square tower and pointed wooden steeple. After suffering severe damage from Hurricane Betsy in 1965, it was demolished and replaced by a high-rise home for the elderly. A Fourth Presbyterian Church, built in 1860, was a long-time landmark at South Liberty and Cleveland streets. After the war, it was purchased by the American Missionary Association for its black flock, and renamed the Central Congregational Church. A guidebook of the 1880s called it "one of the finest churches worshiped in by the colored people in the country." In 1935 it suffered the familiar fate: it was razed and replaced by a parking lot.

There was still another important religion in New Orleans, one that had no official church or meeting place, no salaried clergy, and no official status, and yet had thousands of followers. Voodoo, a potent mixture of African animism, witchcraft, and traces of Christianity, came to New Orleans from the Caribbean, most significantly during the period of the Santo Domingan uprisings. Voodoo rites were performed in out-of-the-way shacks in the poorest sections of New Orleans. Exactly what went on at these ceremonies is hard to identify, since those who really understood them were not likely to confide in white journalists, or — being illiterate — to write their own reports. For many years, the high priestess of Voodoo was Marie Laveau, a woman of color who is buried in St. Louis Number One. Her tomb is easy to find: not only is it kept in good repair and stands out among broken, weedy ones, but it is scribbled with messages of petition and thanks. Voodoo is far from dead in modern New Orleans.

This painting, which hangs in the Cabildo, shows a yacht race on Lake Pontchartrain. The Southern Yacht Club (far right) was built in 1878.

7

"This Great Southern Babylon"

PLACES OF ENTERTAINMENT

"Dissipation in New-Orleans is unlimited," declared the author of *Evans' Pedestrious Tour,* in 1818. Like most newcomers from the northern states, Evans was easily shocked. But even the worldly and sophisticated were astonished by "this great Southern Babylon" (the phrase used in 1836 by James D. Davidson, a critical visitor), where it seemed that the entire population liked to drink, gamble, duel, go to the theater, dance, and bet on the horses — and on Sundays as well as weekdays. Yet as soon as the new regime was well established there seemed little doubt that it was neither the Creoles nor the foreign French who were so rapidly increasing the number of public amusements in New Orleans. It was the Americans.

"One might suppose amid the ravages of disease and death a man would think seriously and live soberly," wrote A. A. Parker of New Hampshire, while visiting New Orleans. Instead, it seemed to him that danger only made New Orleanians more reckless. "But," he added optimistically, "here the career of the debauchee is short. The poisonous atmosphere soon withers and wastes away his polluted life's blood."

Protestants, particularly the New England variety, were distressed by the spectacle of Sunday amusements. Most of them had never been in a Catholic city before. "The state of society [in New Orleans] is very deplorable," wrote a Hartford clergyman in 1814. "The Sabbath to them is a high holiday and on it, is committed, perhaps, more actual sin, than during the whole week besides. Dancing, gambling, parties of pleasure, theatrical amusements, dining parties, etc. etc. are the common business of the day, after mass in the morning.''

Four years later, Welcome Greene, another New Englander, struck a more hopeful note. ''I am happy in being able to say that New Orleans is much less corrupt, in many particulars, than it used to be. The American population there is rapidly increasing; and New England customs, manners and habits, are there gaining ground. This population will, no doubt, be contaminated; but it is sincerely hoped that there will be a balance in favour of morality.''

While awaiting just retribution, New Orleanians had a rich choice of sin. One they loved with a passion was the theater; and throughout the nineteenth century the most important performers of the London and New York stage included New Orleans on their tours. Fanny Elssler, Ellen Tree, Tyrone Power, Charlotte Cushman, Edwin Forrest, Joseph Jefferson, Lola Montez, and all the Booths (Edwin, Junius Brutus, and John Wilkes) were a few of those who braved long journeys by sailing ship or riverboat to reach the flamboyant city on the Mississippi.

New Orleans' first theater was built in 1791. An unpretentious little place, of which no pictures are known to have survived, it stood on St. Peter Street, and was built for a company of refugees from Santo Domingo, who performed in French on a stage so narrow that there was no room for scenery beyond a painted backdrop. In 1810, American entrepreneurs built the St. Philip Street Theater, where patrons might watch plays in English. A second French-language theater, the Orleans, was built in 1809, promptly burned down, and was built again, this time to remain a favorite of Creole audiences throughout the ante-bellum years. It had a ballroom next to it ''in which hitherto most of the Terpsichorian gaieties of our city have had their scene [as a local newspaper put it]. Nothing can exceed the decorum and quiet of the audience except the brilliance of the dress circle, which on certain occasions is completely filled with the beautiful ladies of our city in full evening costume.'' On Mardi Gras, the pit was floored over for dancing, at which time it was ''a coup d'oeil not to be surpassed in effect in America.'' In 1854, the architect Thomas Wharton wrote in his diary that part of the upper galleries had given way, killing five people. ''This fact pleads eloquently against the desecration of the Sabbath by the wretched custom of keeping the theatres open.'' Furthermore, he added, ''it also speaks loudly against

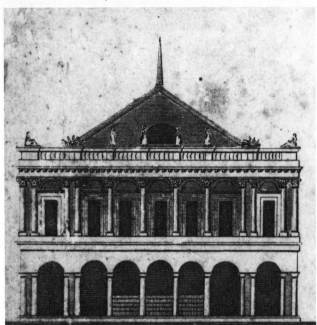

The French cartographer Jacques Tanesse embellished his 1817 plan of New Orleans with drawings of principal buildings, among them these two early theaters. The St. Philip Street Theater, built in 1810, catered to English-speaking audiences, who were then in the minority. At the Orleans Theater, the performances were in French. Next door to it was the Orleans Ballroom, which later became famous — or notorious — for quadroon balls.

the detestable parsimony which directs the construction of buildings designed for the reception of an enthusiastic and often overflowing audience.''

When in 1823 James Caldwell, an English-born entrepreneur who arrived in the city by way of Virginia, built a theater on Camp Street, people laughed at him for choosing a spot in the new Faubourg St. Mary, accessible only over flatboat gunwales laid on top of the mud. Female theatergoers, determined to see the latest play even on a wet night, are said to have taken off their dainty shoes and picked their way over the gunwales in bare feet. Slaves preceded them, carrying lanterns, and others followed with towels and buckets of water. Caldwell, according to an early guidebook, was ''derided as a madman; but how soon was this isolated building surrounded by wealth, beauty and fashion!'' The fact was that Caldwell had money invested in real estate in Faubourg St. Mary and he was well aware that a popular theater would help the area develop. He also owned the gas company, and he made his theater the first in New Orleans to be lit by gas, thereby enhancing the theater's attractions and simultaneously advertising his product. The theater on Camp Street, sometimes called the American Theater, continued in business until 1839, when it was refurbished as a ballroom. Later, it became Armory Hall. It had an attractive Greek Revival facade that survived the changes inside, but eventually the whole structure was razed.

These early theaters were small and simple, but in 1835 James Caldwell built the largest and most splendid one yet seen in the United States, the St. Charles Theater, costing more than $350,000. The architect was the Italian stage designer Antonio Mondelli who had been designing the scenery at the theater on Camp Street, and the new St. Charles was an extravaganza that must have had very much the look of a stage set. The facade included tiers of Corinthian and Ionic columns and a pediment adorned with bas-relief. The interior, which could accommodate 4000, was lavishly fitted with damask draperies, mahogany paneling, and imitation marble. The pièce de résistance was a two-ton chandelier, specially ordered from London, with more than 23,000 cut-glass drops and 250 gaslights. Adding to the glitter were mirrored panels on all the boxes. Each box seated twelve and had its own little reception room, where champagne might be served and people might sit and chat as an alternative to watching the play. Boxes in the lower three tiers cost $1000 for a season's subscription. As in all New Orleans theaters, free persons of color sat in a special upper tier, and so-called African Negroes (blacks with little or no white blood, nearly all of them slaves) were admitted to the highest gallery. The St. Charles became the favorite theater of the American population as soon as it opened and even attracted some of the aloof Creoles who up to that point had seldom ventured across Canal Street. But because of its large size, the St. Charles was not often filled to capacity.

One performer who attracted standing-room-only crowds was Jenny Lind. In February 1851, Jenny, her impresario P. T. Barnum, and their entourage arrived by ship from Havana. By invitation of the Baroness Pontalba they stayed in the then brand-new Pontalba buildings on Jackson Square. A large crowd gathered outside as soon as the singer arrived — and sang to her all evening. The agenda called for several concerts, and, according to a rather curious system worked out by Barnum, tickets for each were sold at auction on the day before. Most of the concerts were sellouts, with patrons coming from as far away as Little Rock to hear the Swedish Nightingale. According to an account by C. G. Rosenberg, one of Barnum's henchmen, "the audience were not disposed altogether blindly to receive and adopt the verdict of New York respecting Jenny's excellence. They were there to hear her with their own ears, and not to take her up on trust on the score of her past successes. At the commencement of the concert they struck me as being cold — colder, indeed, than I had possibly yet seen." But they were soon cheering and applauding.

While Jenny held forth at the St. Charles Theater, Barnum lectured on temperance at the new Lyceum Hall, down the block. He, too, attracted large audiences, because (according to Rosenberg) "in New Orleans, indeed, drinking seems to hold its chief abiding place in the New World."

As for drama, public taste in New Orleans was generally undemanding and the most simple-minded melodrama found favor as long as it was lively. The novels of Sir Walter Scott were an abundant source of material, providing Gothic blood and thunder in either French or English. Audiences got a lot for their money: a full-length play, followed by a shorter afterpiece, generally a farce. With intermissions, an evening at the theater might last five or six hours.

New Orleans had very few native-born performers. One who became famous on two continents was Ada Mencken, best known for her startling interpretation of Mazeppa, Byron's hero of the steppes. Clad in flesh-colored tights and little else, she made her third-act entrance tied to a galloping horse. Ada Mencken was famous from Paris to San Francisco, but because of a rumor that she was the daughter of a free man of color, she appeared only once on the New Orleans stage and never returned.

Theaters were particularly vulnerable to fire because of their many open gas and candle flames, inflammable scenery and costumes, and audiences of smokers. The splendid St. Charles burned down in 1842, but a second one rose on the same spot. The fittings inside were less spectacular than the previous ones, except for a new painted curtain, which showed Shakespeare borne upward in a shower of light on the wings of an American eagle. This St. Charles survived until the end of the century, but by that time its fashionable audiences had deserted it and it was shabby and run-down. It burned, possibly as the result of arson, in 1899. A third theater of the same name, designed by the local firm of Favrot and Livaudais, was built on the same site and lasted until 1967, when it was replaced by a parking lot.

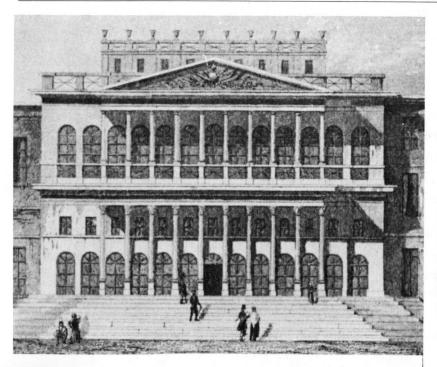

Left top and bottom. When the St. Charles Theater was built in 1835 (on St. Charles between Natchez and Poydras) it was the grandest theater in the United States. Its architect, Antonio Mondelli, took his inspiration from the San Carlos Theater in Naples, which was the third-largest theater in Europe. After the St. Charles burned in 1842, it was rebuilt in less elaborate fashion. The interior shown here is that of the second St. Charles.

Top right. This fine theater on Canal Street was built in 1871–72 as the Varieties, incorporating the facade of one of the old Union Terrace houses (see page 84). Later it became the Grand Opera House. It was demolished in 1906.

Bottom right. This 1861 advertisement for the Academy of Music shows that the management deserved high marks for its interest in new technology, whatever the quality may have been of ''Peculiar Entertainments Involving the services of 200 Artists.'' Costa's Patent Sun-Light seems an effort toward indirect lighting, Demphill's Patent Wind Mill sounds like rudimentary air-conditioning, and central heating was perhaps the purpose of Raymond's Hot Water Chambers.

There were other memorable theaters of the ante-bellum years. The New American Theater was near Lafayette Square. Its seats could be moved in a matter of hours to turn the interior into an arena, suitable for spectacles involving horses, which, in the 1850s, were a very popular form of entertainment. The more horses, the more the public loved it. One spectacle, originally devised by Barnum for the New York stage, began with the Retreat from Moscow and ended with the Battle of Waterloo. It was a smash success when it was put on at the New American. This theater lasted only about as long as the fad for equestrian spectacles; it burned to the ground in 1854. Arson was suspected, as it sometimes was in the case of theaters that hadn't been doing well.

Another enterprise of James Caldwell was the Varieties Theater, built in 1848 on Gravier Street. It had its own stock company. Only four years later it burned and was replaced by a second Varieties, which, in turn, met the usual fate in the 1870s. A third theater of the same name was built on Canal Street, behind the facade of one of Dakin's Union Terrace houses. In 1888, this theater, which had cost $320,000 and was one of the most elaborate in the South, had its name changed to the Grand Opera House and as such it flourished through the 1890s. In 1906, the Maison Blanche department store next door bought and demolished the theater, and erected its present building on the site.

The Academy of Music, originally built to accommodate circuses, was done over in 1855 as a playhouse. At one time it had a museum and a lecture room as well as an auditorium, and advertised that it was heated

Above. The French Opera House stood at the corner of Bourbon and Toulouse streets in the French Quarter. Designed by the firm of Gallier & Esterbrook, it had its gala opening in May 1859 — just two years before the end of New Orleans' glittering ante-bellum era. Although it was not nearly as large as the St. Charles Theater, it was elegant and gracious and New Orleanians immediately took it to their hearts. The auditorium was considered "the finest proportioned ever designed in this city." On special occasions, such as Mardi Gras, the seats in the pit were removed and splendid balls held here on a temporary dance floor. The costume ball shown here took place on Washington's Birthday in 1864, during the Union occupation.

Right. An innovation on the part of the architects of the French Opera House, at least for the French Quarter, was to set the structure back and allow more space in front. A balcony with an iron railing jutted out above the entrance and protected the coiffures of ladies and the silk hats of gentlemen arriving on rainy nights. In the basement there were nine shops that catered to the carriage trade.

in winter and cooled in summer by means of "steam apparatus." In the 1870s it featured seats that were "patent iron settees." Jewell's *Crescent City Illustrated* declared it "one of the cosiest and most elegant places of

amusement in the country." After a short period at the turn of the century under a new name, the Audubon, it burned in February 1903.

The most renowned and beloved of all New Orleans theaters was the French Opera House, which was built in 1859 at the corner of Bourbon and Toulouse streets. The plain but imposing Greek Revival building by Gallier and Esterbrook had a seating capacity of 1600 and room for a thousand standees. In 1859, there were no fire laws governing blocked corridors and aisles, but the French Opera House was better prepared for quick exits than most theaters of the time, having several staircases and many windows. The stage was framed in Corinthian columns. Latticed boxes fronted on the stage and were in demand by ladies who were pregnant and wished to see without being seen. On the second floor was an elaborately furnished saloon or "crush-room" for intermission time as well as a private clubroom for stockholders of the theater, "rooms for the retirement of ladies" and "a range of water-closets." (The quotations are taken from an article in the New Orleans *Delta* on the occasion of the grand opening in May 1859.) Facilities for the actors included a rehearsal theater on the top floor, a green room, and other amenities — for the French Opera House was designed to attract performers of the first caliber, and did so for nearly three-quarters of a century. Then, on the night of December 4, 1919, a fire that originated backstage completely gutted the building. The site is now occupied by the Downtowner Motor Inn.

•

In summer the theaters closed, as they became altogether too hot and uncomfortable. There were no outdoor theaters — perhaps because of the mosquitoes — but a few "pleasure gardens" flourished briefly. During the 1840s, someone tried to carry out Lafon's original intent to have a pleasure garden called Tivoli in what is now Lee Circle. There were outdoor tables, lamps, and shell walks (paths surfaced with tiny white shells) as well as a dance floor and a brass band. For five cents, the band would play a waltz that lasted ten minutes.

When a shell road was built through the swamp to Lake Pontchartrain, people who could afford carriages began to make day excursions to the lakeshore. After 1831, it was also possible to get there by Smoky Mary, the Pontchartrain Railroad's little train. And after the New Canal was finished, one could go by barge. The distance was six miles. One visitor in the 1830s reported that the train trip was made in less than nineteen minutes. "We flew along the track with breathless rapidity . . . We were flying through the fenceless, uninhabited marshes, where nothing meets the eye but dwarf trees, rank, luxuriant undergrowth, tall, coarse grass and vines . . ." Returning, the train encountered a cow on the track, "with a jump-jump and a grinding crash, and with so violent a shock as nearly to throw the car from the track."

In 1849, Harriet Martineau made the excursion by carriage. She passed

cypress, flowering reeds, fleurs-de-lys of every color, palmetto, and a hundred aquatic shrubs new to the eye of the stranger. The gray moss common in damp situations floats in streams from the branches. Snakes abound, and coil about the negroes who are seen pushing their canoes through the rank vegetation, or towing their rafts laden with wood along the sluggish bayou . . . The winding white road is thronged with carriages, driven at a very rapid rate, and full of families of children or gay parties of young people, or a company of smoking merchants, going to the lake to drink or bathe.

The lakeshore became dotted with cottages, built on stilts in the water, and bathing facilities. Mixed bathing — or promiscuous bathing, as those who disapproved were likely to call it — was always the custom at Lake

Another view of the Southern Yacht Club, which was built on pilings in the shallow waters of Lake Pontchartrain.

In the eighteenth century, the French rulers of New Orleans built a fort on Lake Pont-chartrain. It was kept up by the Spanish and for a short time by the Americans, but in the late 1800s it became ruinous. A park was made there, attracting picnickers and Sunday recreationists. Some of the ruins, known as Spanish Fort, are still standing. The old casino (left) and the German beer-garden (right), which was on the other side of Bayou St. John, vanished long ago.

Pontchartrain. Indeed, the presence of gentlemen was considered necessary, in case a lady should be overpowered by the wavelets of the lake and require rescuing.

In the 1870s, the Southern Yacht Club brought wealth and sophistication to the lakeshore and dotted the brown waters with billowing sails. And in the 1890s, outdoor tables and a bandstand at a German beer garden called Over the Rhine did a rousing business from April to November.

The ruins of the old fort built by the Spanish to guard the city from the rear became the nucleus of a public park.

Riverboat outings provided an agreeable diversion in warm weather — unless the captain was addicted to a little diversion of his own, racing, which could turn a pleasant excursion into a deadly nightmare. On July 6, 1852, two excursion boats, the *St. James* and the *California,* entered into one of those irresistible races. The *St. James* exploded, killing many of its passengers outright and tossing others into the Mississippi. To compound the horror, a lifeboat filled with women was run down by the *California,* drowning all but one. Riverboat accidents resulting in multiple deaths and maimings were far from rare.

Riverboats had their own style of decoration, both inside and outside, and they tried to outdo one another in ostentatious flamboyance. When they lay tied up along the levee they looked like two-story houses, as one observer noted, with ''beautiful galleries running round them, so that

A Currier & Ives view of steamboats on the Mississippi, made in 1865. After the Civil War, steamboat traffic revived, but, because of railroad competition, it never returned to the level of ante-bellum days.

when many of them are lying together you might think you had a town before you.''

New Orleans was famous for its public balls, which were on a scale not known elsewhere in the United States. The first American governor of Louisiana, William C. C. Claiborne, had been at his post only a few days when he wrote to his superior, Secretary of State James Madison:

On my arrival at New Orleans, I found the people very Solicitous to maintain their Public Ball establishment . . . The Public Ballroom has been the Theatre of great disorder. During the Winter Season, there has for many years been a Ball twice a week. Every white Male visits it who will pay at the door fifty Cents, and the Ladies of every Rank attend these assemblies in great numbers. The Consequence is that the company is generally composed of a very heterogeneous mass. To keep order at these Balls [under the Spanish regime] a strong guard was stationed at the Ballroom, and on the first appearance of disorder the persons concerned were committed.

Claiborne, though clearly nervous about the prospect of controlling these gatherings, realized that they must continue or he would have worse trouble on his hands. The custom was a Spanish one, found also in other Spanish-American towns such as Santa Fe and San Antonio. Claiborne gave orders that the balls were to continue, but the Creoles continued to be hard to please: In 1811, when the tremors of an earthquake disturbed the dancers at a ball, an old Creole gentlemen was heard to remark that in the days of the Spanish and the French the ladies' pleasure had never been interfered with like this.

The duke of Saxe-Weimar spent several months in New Orleans during the 1830s and apparently enjoyed himself. "No day passed this winter which did not produce something pleasant and interesting," he wrote. "Dinner, evening parties, masquerades and other amusements followed close on each other . . . Tuesdays and Fridays were the nights for the subscription balls, where none but good society were admitted. The ladies are very pretty, with a genteel French air, their dress extremely elegant, after the latest Paris fashion; they dance elegantly."

Balls for children were regularly held at ballrooms early in the evening. Both French and American children from four years old and up attended, but seldom mingled. The little French girls were easy to distinguish, for they wore their hair coiffed like grownups' and were more elaborately and exquisitely dressed than the little Americans.

Quadroon balls, New Orleans' unique and notorious institution, were held until the eve of the Civil War. Some descriptions of them are enthusiastic, some shocked and disgusted. What remains clear is that the women at these balls were all "of color" and were often beautiful, well-dressed and charming, and were sometimes as educated as most white girls, which was not saying a lot. The men who attended the balls had to be white. Some of them only wanted to dance and flirt. Others had come to find a mistress and when they were particularly taken by a lovely quadroon they would negotiate with her mother for the privilege of setting the young woman up in a cottage of her own — usually along Rampart

Street — where the man would have exclusive visitation rights. A girl in these circumstances was called *placée,* and the relationship sometimes continued for years, even after the man married and had legitimate children. Until 1850, when it was outlawed, *plaçage* was legally recognized and the *placées* had certain specific rights. Men sometimes provided well for their children "of color," even sending them to France to be educated, where the schools were better and racial prejudice less of a burden. Some observers, however, derided the idea that there was any decorum about a Quadroon ball, claiming that they were rowdy and frequented by prostitutes. One outraged visitor from the north reported seeing "two females promenading in their night garments." Undoubtedly some were dignified and some were rowdy, but, in any event, the custom persisted until the Civil War. The Orleans Ballroom, where many of these balls were held,

---

In ante-bellum days there were ballrooms all over town — grand or simple, respectable or bawdy. This one, shown in a Notarial Archives watercolor drawing, was of the simpler variety. From November to May, masquerade balls were frequent. George Buckingham, an English visitor, noted, "During our stay, there were three in each week, Tuesday, Thursday, and Sunday; and those who frequented them were usually persons retiring from the theatres at twelve, and remaining at the masquerade till daylight, that on Sunday being always the most thronged."

was acquired in 1881 by the Convent of the Holy Family, an order of nuns "of color." The convent remained there until 1963, when the sisters sold the property to a motel and moved to Chef Menteur Highway.

Slaves were not permitted in ballrooms (unless, perhaps, to play the fiddle), but from colonial times until the 1850s they were allowed to congregate in Congo Square (now Beauregard Square) on Sunday afternoons and dance to their own African or African-derived music. What must have been fascinating performances of authentic West African dances were not much appreciated by contemporary whites, who had no taste for such things. Benjamin Latrobe, watching five or six hundred dancers, thought the whole affair "brutally savage and at the same time dull and stupid." Henry Castellanos, a New Orleanian who wrote in the 1890s of his boyhood memories, used words like "hubbub," "unnatural contortions," and "ridiculous capers." He added, "What made these dances so odd and peculiar was the vibratory motions of the by-standers, who in different styles contributed to the lascivious effect of the scene."

Castellanos also described a game called raquettes, which the blacks had learned from the Choctaws. It was played with a ball about two inches in diameter, which had to be maneuvered with raquettes, shaped like spoons. Opposing teams tried to toss the ball from player to player and eventually through a paper frame suspended between goal posts. The playing field, part of a meadow near Elysian Fields, was half a mile long. "Wrestling and throwing one another down," Castellanos explained, "constituted part of the exercises."

From about 1845 until the Civil War, because of fear of insurrection, the laws governing blacks became more rigid, and both dancing and games were restricted.

Also in the vicinity of Congo Square, a visitor in the early nineteenth century spotted something that sounds very much like a merry-go-round: "a horizontal fandango of four wooden horses, sorrel, white, bay, and black, each pendent by an iron rod, and affixed to stout wheel-machinery in the centre." A less attractive form of amusement that used to take place in Congo Square was the Congo Circus. The specialty here was animal fights: a bull or a bear against dogs, or a bear against a tiger. A typical advertisement read, "If the Tiger is not vanquished in his fight with the Bear, he will be sent alone against the last Bull, and if the latter conquers all his enemies, several pieces of fire-works will be placed on his back, which will produce a very entertaining amusement."

An animal fight was an occasion for betting, but only one among a great variety of such occasions. "The gambling houses in this city are almost innumerable," remarked Estwick Evans, in his *Pedestrious Tour,* "and at any hour, either by night or day the bustle of these demoralizing establishments may be heard." Much gambling centered at the racetracks. One of these was on the site of present Metairie Cemetery, which is laid out in an ellipse, following the shape of the old racetrack. The finest of thoroughbreds were to be seen there as well as (according to a visitor just before the Civil War) "ladies of the highest standing in society."

The city was full of gambling houses. Most bars and coffeehouses had rooms for gambling upstairs or at the back. "In some streets," wrote one traveler, "you can hardly pass a door, or corner, but you will see a party sitting at some game." Bars were often euphemistically called coffee-houses, offering all manner of stimulating beverages, but not much coffee. Cocktails (which were invented in New Orleans), cobblers, juleps, cold punches, and lemonade were in demand in summer, and a slight nip in the air outside brought demands for hot toddies and flaming neguses. Barroom etiquette called for treating and being treated, and then treating again.

So much drinking probably quickened tempers, for quarrels, fistfights, knifings, and duels were common. "Should a stranger jostle an American by accident," commented James Logan, a visitor from Scotland, in 1838, "he runs extreme risk of being shot or stabbed." And an Englishman of about the same period wrote, "I witnessed a personal conflict in which I suppose one of the parties was dirkd. These things are of every-day occurrence; and it is not often that they are taken cognizance of by the police." Dirks might do for the lower classes, but gentlemen preferred to massacre one another by dueling with swords or pistols. Duels were commonly held in what is now City Park, under the "dueling oaks," some of which still stand. The custom continued in New Orleans until the Civil War, although, as one chronicler tells us cheeringly, by that time there were far fewer duels than there had been earlier — not more than fifty a year. Even after the war there were tradition-minded men who insisted on dueling, and these were likely to repair to a bar and beer garden called the Half-Way House. This establishment was halfway to the lakeshore, in Metairie. In the 1890s, it moved to the east side of the New Basin Canal and became a mecca for fans of early jazz.

Perhaps the high incidence of duels was at least partly due to the great number of single men with time on their hands. Those who did not care for dueling, gambling, drinking, or the theater had one splendid alterna-

Bars, restaurants, and coffeehouses were an important part of city life. Unlike modern bars, which favor dim lighting, old-time bars in New Orleans kept the premises as bright as possible. Thom Anderson's in Storyville had a hundred electric light bulbs in its ceiling. The French Quarter bar shown here, circa 1915, seems to be well provided with lights, and also with bartenders, who shucked oysters and dispensed free lunches in addition to pouring drinks. Note the customer, second from right, who must have persuaded the photographer to render him incognito.

tive: eating. New Orleans began to be famous for good food well before the war. Its cooks had an abundance of wonderful ingredients — such as crawfish, pompano, crab, game birds, citrus fruit, pineapple, bananas, and fresh vegetables most of the year — and they knew what to do with them. They had the meticulous standards of French cooking to live up to as well as certain exotic touches supplied by the Spanish and Spanish America (rice and tomato dishes, saffron, cumin, and hot peppers); some contributions from Africa (yams, peanuts, okra), along with the skill and imagination of African-American cooks; plus an important filip from the

Left. This photograph was taken in the last days of Solari's, once known far and wide for its delicacies, which were sold both in a retail shop and at a lunch counter. The building, which was on Royal Street, was torn down in 1961 and replaced by a new structure, housing a parking garage.

Above. St. Patrick's Hall was built in 1866 on Lafayette Square, on the site of the first Odd Fellows Hall, which had burned down. This building lasted until 1914, when it was replaced by the old post office, now the Fifth Circuit Court of Appeals building.

Indians, filé powder. No wonder so many Americans, the majority of whom had subsisted all their lives on a diet that centered on cornmeal and pork, were willing to risk epidemic and flood to settle in New Orleans.

Some time-honored restaurants, notably Antoine's and Maylie's, are still in operation. Others, equally famous in their time, have gone the way of lost New Orleans. Solari's on Royal Street was one, Gluck's was another, and there were many more. Bars and coffeehouses did not offer full-course meals, but they did provide a bewildering outlay of snacks, such as oysters, poor boy sandwiches, pickled eggs, cold shrimp in spicy sauces, and gumbo. An account of the Museum Coffeehouse, written in the 1840s, described it as "illuminated, and enlivened by a band of mu-

Left. This fortresslike Masonic Temple, built in 1891, dominated the corner of St. Charles and Perdido streets until 1926, when it was replaced by the present Masonic Temple.

Above. James Gallier, Jr., was the architect for the Mechanics Institute, built in 1855–56 on University Place as headquarters for the New Orleans Mechanics Society. That organization, founded in 1806, had a large membership, including many ironworkers. In July 1866, the Mechanics Institute was the scene of the most violent incident of the Reconstruction years, when a parade of freedmen, demonstrating for black suffrage, was fired on by police. Thirty-four blacks were killed and 119 wounded.

Left. The Choctaw Club was a political organization with headquarters in a house built by James Gallier in 1841. The elaborate ironwork, added later, was a familiar sight on Lafayette Square until the building was destroyed in the early 1970s.

Above. This quasi-Romanesque building on lower St. Charles Avenue was erected in 1896. For years it was the Harmony Club (a Jewish social organization); then it became the YMHA; and then, when this picture was taken in the 1920s, the offices of Standard Oil of Louisiana. It was razed in the 1950s and has been replaced by an apartment house.

sicians, on every evening. It is a splendid resort, with a small, but choice collection of stuffed birds, and some minerals, in glass cases.'' Alcoholic drinks were considerably more plentiful than coffee.

From an early date, societies, unions, and men's organizations of all kinds had no trouble finding members in New Orleans. In 1853, the Odd Fellows built a handsome, domed headquarters on Lafayette Square, but it soon burned down. St. Patrick's Hall, built on the same site, survived until 1905. The Elks and the Masons had more than one substantial building. In the 1850s, the Mechanics Institute acquired its headquarters, which figured in the city's political history during Reconstruction, and for a time housed the Fisk Free Library.

After the Civil War, the London and New York idea of private and exclusive clubs caught on quickly among the gentlemen of New Orleans' establishment. Wishing to avoid racially mixed public places and, espe-

Left. The building with the balustraded roof was the Pickwick Club at 1030 Canal Street. It was built in 1896 by the Boston firm of Shepley, Rutan and Coolidge, successors to the famous Louisiana-born architect Henry Hobson Richardson. The Pickwick Club has moved and its once fashionable clubhouse is barely recognizable. The ground floor has been destroyed and houses a shoe store. The side entrance has two stories built on top of it, and the brick facade has been painted.

Below. The Washington Artillery on Camp Street was for years the scene of military drills and balls, and of the Rex Mardi Gras ball.

cially, carpetbaggers, those who could afford it abandoned public bars and did their drinking among their peers. During the late nineteenth century and the turn-of-the-century years, several club headquarters were built or acquired, but today only the Boston Club still occupies the building it has had since 1884, the only former private residence surviving on Canal Street. Military organizations, such as the Washington Artillery, also built their own halls, where they drilled and held dress parades and balls. All these clubs and organizations added a great deal to the city's social life, particularly at Mardi Gras time.

•

To think of Mardi Gras is to think of New Orleans, and vice versa. Pre-Lenten festivities began with the first French colonists, and, if anything, were increased and encouraged by the Spanish. The great majority of

Above. On a rainy Mardi Gras, circa 1890, a mule-drawn float dazzles the crowd along a downtown street.

Right. On Mardi Gras, the fashionable clubs along Canal Street built grandstands and went in for lavish illumination. These pictures show the Pickwick Club (left) and the Chess, Checkers and Whist Club (right) awaiting the crowds and the parades.

Americans, after recovering from their predictable shock, took up the custom with enthusiasm. There was never a year without some sort of Mardi Gras celebration, but occasionally these were marred by rowdiness and even violence. The year 1857 was the first in which a group of citizens took it upon themselves to organize a theme, pageant, and tableaux, an innovation that proved immensely successful and is still followed.

After the Civil War and the grimmest years of Reconstruction, Mardi Gras had a renaissance. It became more elaborate than ever, with balls and parades beginning two or three weeks in advance of Fat Tuesday itself. In the 1870s it took on its modern trappings: its incredibly imagi-

native and costly costumes, its "Krewes" (members of Mardi Gras organizations), its Queen and Maids, and the custom of riders on floats throwing baubles to the crowd. The rites of a New Orleans Mardi Gras seem esoteric indeed to an outsider. Membership in the older organizations — Comus, Rex, Momus, Proteus, the Twelfth Night Revelers, and, for blacks, the Zulu (Zulu Social Aid and Pleasure Club) — is for the establishment only, and highly coveted. In the eyes of New Orleans girls, to be Queen of Carnival is scarcely a lesser position than being Queen of England. In recent years, more organizations have sprung up, so that almost any eager citizen can find one to belong to, although membership is by invitation. For years, the floats were mule-drawn, mounted on wagons or garbage trucks. Now they are motorized, each one costing thousands of dollars, and the parades take place day and night over the two weekends before the final Tuesday. And then, on Ash Wednesday, countless plastic jewelled necklaces and colored feathers and masks and bits of finery strew the city as if it were a gigantic stage and the curtain has just come down on an extravaganza, a follies, and a circus, all in one.

Some of the settings for Mardi Gras festivities no longer exist: for example, the old ferry station at the foot of Canal Street, where a stand-in for Rex used to disembark from a yacht on the day before Mardi Gras and proceed to city hall to receive the keys to the city from the mayor. The French Opera House, where the most exclusive balls of the season used to be held, no longer stands, and since the old Pickwick Club on Canal Street was turned into a shoe store, the Comus maids of honor watch the Comus parade from the present Pickwick Club at Canal and St. Charles. But the spirit that animates these extraordinary festivities is in no danger of becoming part of lost New Orleans; as long as the city exists, it will have Mardi Gras.

There were (and still are) other traditional Creole holidays besides Mardi Gras: New Year's Day, a great day for exchanging presents and social calls; and All Saints Day, November 1, the time for visiting the cemeteries. Native New Orleanians, black and white, have always liked holidays and they found no difficulty in helping the incoming Americans celebrate the holidays they brought with them, such as the Fourth of July, Washington's Birthday, and Thanksgiving. One holiday that became, in New Orleans, like a second Fourth of July was the Eighth of January. On that day, speeches and parades in Jackson Square still celebrate Andrew Jackson's victory over the British in 1815 at the Battle of New Orleans. The battlefield itself, just down the river at Chalmette, is now a National Historical Park.

After the Civil War, the important holiday for blacks was Emancipation Day, to commemorate the day in 1864 when Lincoln proclaimed freedom for the slaves. On June 11 of that year, the Emancipation Proclamation was celebrated in Congo Square. Union troops were occupying the city, and General Banks and other Union officers attended, along with a crowd of 20,000 freedmen. They watched a parade of black regiments, listened to speeches in English and French, and when a chorus of Sunday school children sang a specially composed emancipation song, everyone joined in the refrain:

> So fare you well, poor massa,
> May God Almighty help you;
> I'll never feel your lash again,
> For now we all are free!

New Orleans has had more than one elaborate and costly piece of architecture built in the full knowledge that it would be only temporary.

To honor Andrew Jackson when he returned to the city after his victory at Chalmette, a triumphal arch was quickly erected. It was made of wood and plaster, with six Corinthian pillars and two cherubs at the top. The whole thing was painted to resemble marble. In 1825, when the marquis de Lafayette visited the city at the end of an official tour of the United States, he, too, was honored with a triumphal arch, a municipal brainstorm conceived just two weeks before he was to arrive on April 10. In double-quick time two French residents, a stage designer and an architect, designed and constructed a sixty-eight-foot high wood and canvas arch. A forty-foot base was painted to look like green Italian marble. The upper part was sectioned into twenty-four parts, one for each state, and disguised as yellow Verona marble. Each "marble" block was studded with a gilded bronze star.

Lafayette arrived in a heavy rainstorm aboard the steamboat *Natchez*. A fleet of other steamboats went to meet him. He stood bareheaded on deck, acclaimed by cheers, gun salutes, and the frantic tooting of whistles. After lunching at a downriver plantation, he entered the city riding in a landau drawn by six white horses, while bells rang and the people cheered. The six days of his visit were a continual holiday for New Orleanians, and the old gentleman displayed an iron constitution, surviving two balls; three trips to the theater; several parades; a sightseeing tour of the city; at least a dozen receptions, public and private; and a gala dinner nearly every night. Special accommodations were set up for him in the Cabildo, but, from the sound of it, he spent very little time there.

The remarkable Saengerbundfesthalle was an entire temporary theater erected in 1892 at Lee Circle especially for a festival of the North American Saenger Bund, a national German-American singing club. This organization had been holding regular festivals for a quarter of a century in places where many Germans had settled, such as Milwaukee and St. Louis, but this was their first in New Orleans and the large local population of German extraction went all out to demonstrate Southern hospitality. They raised more than $50,000 through a bond sale in order to finance the festival and build the hall, which could accommodate 6400 spectators and 2000 singers plus an orchestra. Above the stage, an arch of gaslights spelled out the legend NORTH AMERICAN SINGER UNION. Suspended above that was a lyre made of fresh flowers, and at each end "huge stars of gas jets" (according to a newspaper report of opening night). The festival, a triumphant success, lasted less than two weeks. The site of the hall is now occupied by the K&B office building.

Far left. This handsome arch, looking as substantial as Trajan's or Constantine's, was in reality nothing but flimsy wood and canvas and was not intended to last. It was erected in the spring of 1825 in honor of Lafayette's visit to New Orleans and stood sixty-eight feet high in the middle of the Place d'Armes (present-day Jackson Square). The bust on top does not, oddly enough, represent Lafayette, but Benjamin Franklin (being crowned by Wisdom). Following the six-day celebration honoring the illustrious visitor, the arch was dismantled. The drawing shown here was made in 1909.

Left. The Saengerbundfesthalle at Lee Circle was built in 1892 for a two-week singing festival. In the background are the two gilded turrets of Temple Sinai.

Bottom left. This drawing made in 1884 shows the World Industrial and Cotton Centennial Exposition under construction. The street vendor at the left is advertising his wares by blowing a trumpet.

But by far the most ambitious temporary buildings ever constructed in New Orleans were those for the World's Industrial and Cotton Centennial Exposition, which opened in December 1884 on the site of present Audubon Park. As has often been the case with world's fairs and expositions, this one was beset with problems from first to last. Congress had allocated a large sum of money to the city to prepare the exposition, but had stipulated that since it was intended to commemorate the centennial anniversary of the first shipment of cotton from the United States in 1784, the gates must open in 1884. By the end of December, some important features were not ready (including comfort stations, benches, and restaurants) nor was there suitable transportation for fairgoers from the center of town, but the exposition opened anyway. Because of its state of unpreparedness, it got a bad press. Journalists who had come to town for the opening took more interest in a spectacular murder and a violent streetcar strike that happened to occur just then than they did in the rather limp ceremonies of the grand opening. One local newspaper, the *Mascot* (admittedly anti-establishment in its views), called the exposition "a colossal white elephant floundering in the mire of stupidity, mismanagement, and we dare say corruption . . . A monster bazaar of knick-knacks, machinery, and varied commodities, useful and ornamental, interspersed here and there with a small collection of arts and scientific appliances, and called the World's Exposition, which costs almost as much money to house, light, keep and guard as the entire lot is worth."

This was probably all true, and yet there were many delightful and unique features about the exposition. The main building was the largest ever erected anywhere up to that time, covering thirty-three acres, and

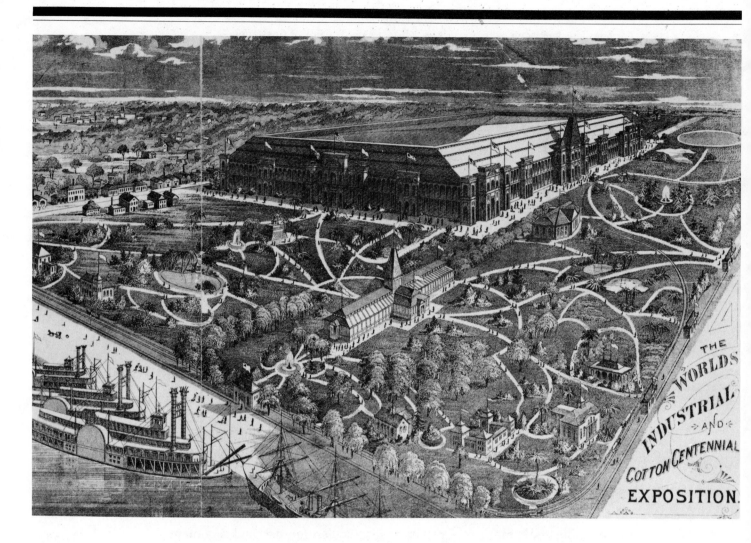

containing twenty-five miles of corridors and walks. In a world where even one elevator in a building was rare, this structure had twenty. In its central part was a music hall large enough for an audience of 11,000 and an orchestra of 600. There was also a fine, large organ, but, unfortunately, after a few weeks it brought down part of the roof. The United States Government building covered twelve acres, and offered exhibits from every department — including "wired and bottled samples of human anatomy" from the Medical Branch of the Army and, from the Justice Department, a hemp noose bearing a sign that read THIS ROPE HAS BEEN USED. The Liberty Bell was lent by Philadelphia, in spite of an outcry on the part of Philadelphians who feared the perfidious Southerners would melt the bell down and make it into a statue of Jefferson Davis.

Left. A bird's-eye view of the exposition grounds, 1885. Fairgoers might arrive via the St. Charles Avenue railway or the steamboat from downtown. To see everything (according to the official exposition guide) one needed "four days for a rapid tour." The tour covered thirty-five miles; it was possible to rent a rolling-chair, or to ride on the electric railway that circled the grounds. The large building in the foreground was Horticultural Hall. It was 600 feet long, the biggest conservatory in the world, but it was completely dwarfed by the huge main building, which measured 1378 feet long by 905 feet wide.

Above. Beautiful Audubon Park, constructed on the fairgrounds after the Cotton Exposition closed, is still there, but it no longer has the swanboats that delighted children for several decades. And a marvelous merry-go-round, with hand-carved horses imported from Germany, was sold into private hands about 1970.

Among other buildings was the Art Gallery made of cast iron and glass and a model cotton factory, showing cotton in every state of processing, including a cotton field outside. Among foreign exhibitors, the Mexicans had the most impressive building, a ziggurat costing $200,000. The Horticultural Hall was billed as the largest conservatory in the world, featuring a twenty-five-foot cactus from Arizona and model gardens typical of California, Florida, and Central America. The building's ninety-foot glass tower was lighted at night, and even the *Mascot* mellowed enough to report that "when illuminated by the white radiance of the electric light . . . [the exposition] lies like a great glowworm amongst the shadows of the soft, odorous Southern night." The Horticultural Hall survived the exposition and became part of Audubon Park, but was demolished by the 1915 hurricane.

Most of the states sent exhibits, such as a Statue of Liberty made of hay and corncobs (from Nebraska), a cathedral of crackerboxes, a Greek temple made of soap, and costumed models of pigs dining on ham. In remarkably modern fashion, minorities were invited to send exhibits, too. There was a Colored People's Exhibit and a Women's Department — the latter presided over by Julia Ward Howe as a gracious gesture of reconciliation with the North on the part of the City of New Orleans. A real Sioux chief, Dakota, and his wife and child were present, living in a wigwam.

The exposition lasted until June 1885, when it closed in financial disarray. Reorganized and given another name, the American Exposition, it reopened in November and continued until March 1886, at which point there was an auction sale and all the buildings except the Horticultural Hall were demolished. Financially, the enterprise had been a failure; but as a boost to post-Reconstruction morale it had value and as an architectural exercise in the making of innovative temporary buildings it was historic.

•

But of all the many forms of entertainment that this lighthearted city has engendered, the most significant, the most original, and, of course, the best known, is jazz. (The word is believed to derive from *jasi,* which in the language of the Mandingo tribe of West Africa means "to act out of the ordinary.") And jazz has very few landmarks. It simply "happened" at parades, funerals, and parties, on the decks of riverboats, and in forgotten social halls, bars, churches, backyards, and bordellos.

 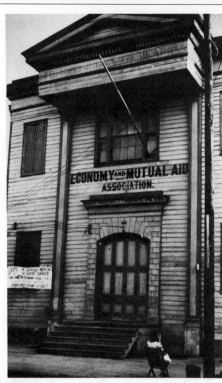 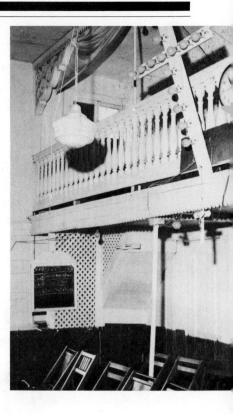

Among the incubation places of early jazz were black social clubs, such as the minuscule premises of the "Society of the Inseperable Friends" (left), and (center and right) the Economy and Mutual Aid Association (known to jazz lovers as Economy Hall).

Jazz has many myths, perhaps the most persistent one being that it originated in Storyville, the city's red-light district, at the turn of the century. It is true that some of the great jazz musicians had jobs there before they moved on to better things, but the music itself came from a number of sources: from African answering chants, such as had formerly been heard in Congo Square; from white folk music; from the musical traditions of New Orleans' persons of color, stemming from both races; and from the work songs of plantation and riverboat hands. For years before anyone knew the word *jazz,* New Orleans had marching brass bands and strolling musicians. One of the few blacks to appear on the stage of a white theater was a street vendor of cornmeal, who sang at the St. Charles in 1837 under the name of Signor Cornmeali. Plantation owners

Above. A ticket on a Streckfus Line riverboat, circa 1918, included a chance of hearing music by some of the greatest names in jazz. Here, left to right: Baby Dodds, Bebe Ridgley, Joe Howard, Louis Armstrong, Fate Marable (leader of the band), David Jones, Johnny Dodds, Johnny St. Cyr, and Pops Foster.

Right. Some of New Orleans' best bands played at the roof garden of the Pythian Temple at Gravier and Saratoga streets. This photograph was taken in August 1923 on opening night after a roof had been added over the dance floor.

sometimes hired music teachers for talented slaves or freedmen, so that the owners might have their own private bands, made up of such instruments as the fiddle, clarinet, drum, flute, tambourine, fife, and triangle. Bands "of color" played at quadroon balls, and some few persons of color were either sent to Paris to study classical music or learned it from members of the French Opera House orchestra.

In New Orleans, which was never a strictly segregated city, blacks often lived in the white neighborhoods where they worked. Downtown, in Faubourg Marigny and elsewhere, were neighborhoods of free persons of color; uptown there were certain all-black neighborhoods, which grew in size after the advent of streetcars to transport workers to and from jobs. The two racial groups rarely mingled until Jim Crow laws were passed in the 1890s, forcing ''coloreds'' and ''American Negroes'' (as blacks were called by ''persons of color'') to share schools and various public accommodations. Whatever the sociological results may have been, the new mixture was an advantage to jazz. Nonwhite bands came to have members of varying degrees of musical sophistication. Among the persons of color, many could read music. Most blacks could not, but they often had a genius for improvisation, one of the most important ingredients of jazz, which, according to Al Rose, one of the founders of New Orleans' Jazz Museum, should be defined as follows: ''Any music played in 2/4 or 4/4 syncopated time by two or more tonal instruments improvising collectively.''

Any student of early jazz knows the names of its first musicians, and they were all from New Orleans: Buddy Bolden, King Oliver, Jelly Roll Morton, Bunk Johnson, Sidney Bechet, Willie the Lion Smith, and Kid

---

All these prim- and proper-looking houses along the railroad tracks on Basin Street were bordellos — the most expensive in New Orleans. At the extreme right is Mahogany Hall, built to the specifications of the formidable octoroon madam Lulu White. The cottage next door (small, but as wicked as the rest) adjoined Josie Arlington's Palace. Farther down the block, the building with pillars in front of it was Tom Anderson's saloon, also known as the Arlington Annex.

Ory — to name only a few; and, of course, the greatest of them all, Louis Armstrong. They played for social occasions at Perseverance Hall, Economy Hall, Funky Butt Hall, and other humble places — nearly all now vanished — along with the grander premises in Storyville. From those origins the music New Orleans created has risen into the air and circled the world. No performer ever attracted such huge, enthusiastic audiences as Louis Armstrong when he toured Europe. "Basin Street Blues," "Didn't He Ramble," "When the Saints Go Marching In," "Mahogany Hall Stomp" — these songs are standard musical fare now in Paris, Moscow, Tokyo, and Sydney; while in Bangkok, the king of Thailand plays jazz, New Orleans style, on the clarinet.

Storyville, New Orleans' red-light district, where several famous jazz musicians got their start, was so named in mock honor of an alderman named Sidney Story, who, in 1897, sponsored a law that restricted prostitution in New Orleans to a few blocks around Basin Street. Before that, ever since the earliest French colonial days, prostitutes had usually had the run of the city. When laws were passed forbidding soliciting in the streets, the girls did so from the windows. In the days of epidemics, whores, like everyone else, were ranked as Go-aways and Can't-get-aways, the latter being the less successful or the has-beens. Soon after 1897, Storyville became divided into an unofficial social hierarchy.

Basin Street was the swanky neighborhood. Facing the railroad tracks, which ran down the street's neutral ground, were lavish houses such as Lulu White's and Josie Arlington's — the latter known to its patrons quite simply as The Palace. Down at the corner of Customhouse and Basin was a famous bar and nightspot known as the Arlington Annex. It was owned by a lover of Josie's, Thomas Anderson, who was in the state legislature. Architecturally, these establishments were massive and showy. Inside, they were marvels of costly bad taste, filled with such treasures as silver doorknobs, mirrors embossed with nudes, and massive mahogany beds. At some of them, customers were not admitted unless dressed in evening clothes, and the fee, which might be put on a charge account, could run as high as a hundred solid early-twentieth-century dollars. In contrast, nearby blocks were lined with sordid cribs, which slumlords rented by the night at exorbitant prices to the more pitiful ladies of the night.

In its heyday, the first decade of this century, Storyville was a remarkable place. It even had a Blue Book which described the girls in roguish double-entendres, such as "Grace has always made it a mark in life to treat everyone alike and to see that they enjoy themselves while in her

Above. In contrast to the tawdry splendors of Basin Street, other blocks in Storyville presented a dismal scene of decrepit old houses that had been turned into cribs. The photograph shows Iberville Street between Marais and Liberty.

Right. This aerial view of Storyville is believed to have been taken from a balloon, circa 1914. Storyville lay between the covered railroad tracks on Basin Street and St. Louis Cemetery Number Two (the larger cemetery in the photograph). Just before World War II, nearly every house was leveled, and a housing project now stands in this area.

midst." But despite the fanciness of its houses and women and its nationwide notoriety (it was the only legal red-light district in the country), the fortunes of Storyville declined. By the time it was officially shut down in 1917, at the insistence of the United States Navy, it was shabby and financially depressed. Just before World War II, almost the entire area,

from Lulu White's Mahogany Hall down to the lowest crib, was demolished to make way for a housing project.

•

The destruction of the palaces of Storyville, as well as the rickety bars and clubs where jazz began, is not to be regretted as far as architecture is concerned. And it could be argued that a number of the lost buildings illustrated in this book were never world-class monuments. Nevertheless, they were part of a great city's history and culture, and some were among the finest examples of their kind. Nothing is gained when buildings of the caliber of the St. Charles Hotel or the Campbell house are replaced with parking lots or cheap, unsightly buildings. Until only a few years ago there was, a real danger that New Orleans would lose its character completely through this mindless demolition, but it is a vigorous city and once the danger to it was apparent, thousands of its citizens came forward to defend it. Just as Andrew Jackson stopped the British, the preservationist associations stopped another kind of defeat, and insured that henceforward there would be constant vigilance against the vandalism of wreckers.

Enough has been lost to make what is left seem precious indeed.

"We walked slowly . . . through many streets of the Old Town, Negro women laughing all around us in the dusk, shadows playing over old buildings, children with their shrill cries dodging in and out of old hallways . . . In a patio back of an old building a Negress sang a French song." — Sherwood Anderson, *Notebook,* 1926.

Notes and Sources
for Illustrations

Bibliography

Index

Notes and Sources for Illustrations

4. "A Palace for Creature Comforts": Hotels

5. Health and Hazards: The Fight Against Disasters

6. Mind and Spirit: Schools, Libraries, and Places of Worship

7. "This Great Southern Babylon": Places of Entertainment

Bibliography

Books

American Institute of Architects, New Orleans chapter. *A Century of Architecture in New Orleans (1857–1957)*, New Orleans, 1957.

Anderson, Sherwood. *Notebook*. New York, 1926.

Anonymous ["By a Resident"]. *New Orleans as It Is*. New Orleans, 1855.

————. ["Semper Idem"]. *Blue Book in New Orleans*. New Orleans, 1936.

Appleton's Companion Handbook of Travel. New York, 1865.

Armstrong, Louis. *Satchmo: My Life in New Orleans*. New York, 1955.

Asbury, Herbert. *The French Quarter*. New York, 1936.

Barton, E. H., M.D. *Temperance and of the Application of Stimulants in a Warm Climate*. New Orleans, 1837.

Basso, Etolia Simmons, ed. *The World from Jackson Square*. New York, 1972.

Berquin-Duvallon [First name unknown]. *Travels in Louisiana and the Floridas, 1802, Giving a Correct Picture of Those Countries*. New York, 1806.

Blasangame, J. *Black New Orleans*. Chicago, 1973.

Bossu, Jean-Bernard. *Travels in the Interior of North America*. Norman, Oklahoma, 1962.

Bremer, Frederika. *Homes of the New World*. Boston, 1847.

Buckingham, James. *The Slave States of America*. 2 vols. London, 1842.

Buntline, Ned [Edward Z. Judson]. *Mysteries and Miseries of New Orleans*. Philadelphia, 184-.

Butler, Major-General Benjamin F. *Butler's Book*. New York, 1893.

Byrnes, James. *Edgar Degas, His Family and Friends in New Orleans*. New York, 1965.

Calhoun, Daisy Breaux. *Autobiography of a Chameleon*. Washington, 1930.

Capers, Gerald. *Occupied City*. Boston, 1865.

Carter, Hodding, and Betty Werlein Carter. *So Great a Good*. Sewanee, Tennessee, 1955.

Carter, Hodding. *The Past as Prelude*. New York, 1968.

Castellanos, Henry C. *New Orleans as It Was*. New Orleans, 1895.

Chase, Philander. *Bishop Chase's Reminiscences*. Boston, 1847.

Clark, John G. *New Orleans, 1718–1812: An Economic History*. Baton Rouge, Louisiana, 1970.

Clements, William Edwards. *Plantation Life on the Mississippi*. New Orleans, 1952.

Cohn, David L. *New Orleans and Its Living Past*. Boston, 1941.

Contractors and Dealers Exchange. *Architectural New Orleans*. New Orleans, 1908.

Curtis, Nathaniel Cortlandt. *New Orleans, Its Old Houses, Shops and Public Buildings*. Philadelphia, 1933.

Darby, William. *A Geographical Description of the State of Louisiana*. Philadelphia, 1816.

Davies, Ebenezer. *American Scenes and Christian Slavery*. London, 1849.

Didimus, Henry [Edward Henry Durrell]. *New Orleans as I Found It*. New York, 1845.

Dowler, Bennett, M.D. *Researches upon the Necropolis of New Orleans*. New Orleans, 1850.

———. *Tableaux Geographical, Commercial, Geological and Sanitary of New Orleans*. New Orleans, 1850–51.

Duffy, John. *Sword of Pestilence*. Baton Rouge, Louisiana, 1966.

Dufour, Charles L. *Ten Flags in the Wind*. New York, 1967.

Du Pratz, Antoine Simon Le Page. *The History of Louisiana*. Baton Rouge, Louisiana, 1975.

Elliott, Maude Howe. *Three Generations*. Boston, 1923.

Emigrants Directory. London, 1820.

Evans, Estwick. *Evans's Pedestrious Tour of Four Thousand Miles Through the Western States and Territories During the Winter and Spring of 1818*. Concord, New Hampshire, 1819.

Fearon, Henry Bradshaw. *A Sketch of America*. London, 1819.

Fitch, James Marston. *Architecture and the Esthetics of Plenty*. New York, 1961.

Flint, Timothy. *Recollections of the Last Ten Years in the Valley of the Mississippi*. Carbondale, Illinois, 1968.

Fremont, Jessie Benton. *Souvenirs of My Time*. Boston, 1887.

Friends of the Cabildo. *New Orleans Architecture*. 6 vols. New Orleans, 1971–78.

Gallier, James. *Autobiography*. New York, 1973.

Galsworthy, John. *The Inn of Tranquillity*. New York, 1919.

Gibson, John. *Gibson's Guide and Directory*. New Orleans, 1838.

Glazier, Captain Willard. *Peculiarities of American Cities*. Philadelphia, 1885.

Goldstein, Moise H. *Architecture of Old New Orleans*. New Orleans, 1902.

Greene, Welcome Arnold. *Journals*. Madison, Wisconsin, 1957.

A. G. Griswold and Company's New Orleans Guide Book. New Orleans, 1873.

Hachard, Marie Madeleine. *Relation du voyage des religieuses Ursulines de Rouen à la Nouvelle-Orléans en 1727*. Rouen, 1865.

Hall, A. Oakey. *The Manhattaner in New Orleans*. New York, 1851.

Hall, Mrs. Basil. *The Aristocratic Journey*. New York, 1961.

Hamlin, Talbot. *Benjamin Henry Latrobe*. New York, 1955.

Hearn, Lafcadio. *Creole Sketches*. Boston, 1924.

Hentoff, Nat. *Jazz*. New York, 1959.

Hosmer, James K. *The Color-Guard*. Boston, 1864.

Houstoun, Mrs. *Texas and the Gulf of Mexico, or Yachting in the New World*. London, 1844.

Howe, William W. *Municipal History of New Orleans*. Baltimore, 1889.

Huber, Leonard. *To Glorious Immortality*. New Orleans, 1961.

———. *New Orleans: A Pictorial History*. New York, 1971.

Hunt, Louise Livingston. *Memoir of Mrs. Edward Livingston*. New York, 1886.

Huxtable, Ada Louise. *Kicked a Building Lately?* New York, 1976.

Ingraham, Joseph Holt. *Southwest by a Yankee.* New York, 1835.

Jackson, Joseph. *Development of American Architecture, 1783–1830.* Philadelphia, 1926.

Jackson, Joy J. *New Orleans in the Gilded Age.* Baton Rouge, Louisiana, 1969.

Jewell, Edwin L. *Crescent City Illustrated.* New Orleans, 1873.

Johnson, Thomas Cary. *Life and Letters of Benjamin Morgan Palmer.* Richmond, Virginia, 1906.

Kendall, John. *A History of New Orleans.* 3 vols. Chicago, 1922.

———. *The Golden Age of the New Orleans Theatre.* Baton Rouge, Louisiana, 1952.

Kerns, J. H. *The Negro in New Orleans.* New Orleans, 1958.

King, Edward. *The Great South.* Hartford, Connecticut, 1875.

King, Grace. *New Orleans: The Place and the People.* New York, 1895.

———. *Memories of a Southern Woman of Letters.* New York, 1932.

Kirsch, Elise. *"Down Town" New Orleans in the Early Eighties.* New Orleans, 1951.

Knight, Henry L. [pseudonym, Arthur Singleton]. *Letters from the South and West.* New York, 1823.

Koch, Albert C. *Journey through a Part of the United States of North America in the Years 1844 to 1846.* Carbondale, Illinois, 1972.

Kreeger, Maurice. *I Remember When.* New Orleans, 1955.

Latrobe, Benjamin H. *Impressions Respecting New Orleans, 1818–1820.* Edited by Samuel Wilson, Jr. New York, 1951.

Latrobe, Charles Joseph. *The Rambler in North America.* London, 1837.

Lewis, Peirce F. *New Orleans — The Making of an Urban Landscape.* Philadelphia, 1977.

Lloyd, W. Alvin. *Steamboat and Railroad Guide.* New Orleans, 1857.

Logan, James. *Notes of a Journey through Canada, the United States of America, and the West Indies.* Edinburgh, 1838.

Lomax, Alan. *Mister Jelly Roll.* New York, 1956.

Lyall, Sir Charles. *A Second Visit to the United States.* London, 1849.

Mackie, J. Milton. *From Cape Cod to Dixie and the Tropics.* New York, 1864.

Major, Howard. *Domestic Architecture of the Early American Republic: The Greek Revival.* Philadelphia, 1926.

Martineau, Harriet. *Retrospect of Western Travel.* London, 1838.

Meeks, Carroll L. V. *The Railroad Station.* New Haven, Connecticut, 1956.

de Montule, Edouard. *Travels in America — 1816–1817.* Bloomington, Indiana, 1951.

Mumphrey, A. *New Orleans Riverfront Expressway.* New Orleans, 1970.

Nau, John Frederick. *The German People of New Orleans, 1850–1900.* Leiden, Holland, 1958.

Needham, Maurice. *Negro Orleanian.* New Orleans, 1962.

New Orleans Press, ed. *Historical Sketch Book and Guide to New Orleans.* New York, 1885.

New Orleans World's Industrial Exposition. *Report of the Woman's Department.* New Orleans, 1885.

Newton, Milton B. *Louisiana House Types.* Museum of Geoscience, Louisiana State University, Baton Rouge, Louisiana, 1971.

Nichols, T. L. *Forty Years of American Life.* Harrisburg, Pennsylvania, 1937.

Nolte, Vincent. *Memoirs.* New York, 1934.

Norman, Benjamin. *Norman's New Orleans and Environs.* New York, 1845.

Ogg, Frederic Austin. *The Opening of the Mississippi.* New York, 1904.

Olmsted, Frederick Law. *A Journey in the Seaboard Slave States.* New York, 1856.

Pfeiffer, Ida. *A Lady's Second Journey Round the World.* London, 1856.

Pickett, Albert J. *Eight Days in New Orleans in February, 1847.* Montgomery, Alabama, 1847.

Pittman, Captain Philip. *The Present State of the European Settlements on the Mississippi.* 1770. Reprint. Cleveland, Ohio, 1906.

Power, Tyrone. *Impressions of America.* London, 1836.

Parker, A. A. *A Trip to the West and Texas.* Concord, New Hampshire, 1836.

Reclus, Elisee. *Le tour du monde: Fragment d'un voyage à la Nouvelle-Orléans.* Paris, 1855.

Reed, Merl E. *New Orleans and the Railroads.* New York, 1966.

Report of the Sanitary Commission of New Orleans on the Epidemic Yellow Fever of 1853. New Orleans, 1854.

Ricciuti, Italo. *New Orleans and Its Environs.* New York, 1938.

Ripley, Eliza. *Social Life in Old New Orleans.* New York, 1912.

Robin, C. C. *Voyages in the Interior of Louisiana (1802–1806).* Translated by Stuart O. Landry, Jr. New Orleans, 1966.

Robinson, William L. *The Diary of a Samaritan.* New York, 1860.

Rohrer, J. H. and M. S. Edmonson. *The Eighth Generation.* New York, 1960.

Rose, Al. *New Orleans Jazz.* New York, 1967.

———. *Storyville, New Orleans.* University of Alabama, University, Alabama, 1974.

Rose, George. *The Great Country.* London, 1868.

Rosenberg, C. G. *Jenny Lind in America.* New York, 1851.

Rousseve, Charles B. *The Negro in New Orleans.* New Orleans, 1969.

Russell, William Howard. *My Diary North and South.* London, 1863.

Sala, George Augustus. *America Revisited.* London, 1885.

Samuel, Ray and Martha Ann Brett Samuel. *The Great Days of the Garden District; and the Old City of Lafayette.* New Orleans, 1961.

Sandburg, Carl. *Abraham Lincoln: The Prairie Years.* New York, 1926.

Sargent, Angelina M. *Notes of Travel.* Rochester, New York, 1904.

Saxe-Weimar-Eisenach, Bernhard, duke of. *Travels Through North America, 1825–26.* Philadelphia, 1828.

Saxon, Lyle. *Fabulous New Orleans.* New York, 1928.

Saxon, Lyle, and Robert Tallant. *Gumbo Ya-Ya.* Boston, 1945.

Saunders, William. *Through the Light Continent.* London, 1879.

Schauffer, Robert Haven. *Romantic America.* New York, 1913.

Schermerhorn, John F. and Samuel J. Mills. *A Correct View of That Part of the United States Which Lies West of the Alleghany Mountains, with Regard to Religion and Morals.* Hartford, Connecticut, 1814.

Scully, Arthur, Jr. *James Dakin.* Baton Rouge, Louisiana, 1973.

Semple, Henry Churchill, S.J. *The Ursulines in New Orleans, 1727–1925.* New York, 1925.

Shapiro, Nat and Nat Hentoff. *Hear Me Talkin' to Ya.* New York, 1955.

Smyth, John. *A Tour in the United States of America.* London, 1784.

Southern, Eileen. *The Music of Black America.* New York, 1971.

Sparks, W. H. *Memories of Fifty Years.* New Orleans, 1872.

Stuart, James. *Three Years in North America.* London, 1833.

The Story of the Jewish Orphans' Home. New Orleans, 1905.

Swanson, Betsy. *Historic Jefferson Parish.* Gretna, La., 1975.

Szarkowski, John, ed. *E. J. Bellocq, Storyville Portraits.* New York, 1970.

Tallant, Robert. *Voodoo in New Orleans.* New York, 1946.

———. *The Romantic New Orleanians.* New York, 1950.

Taylor, Joe Gray. *Louisiana.* New York, 1976.

Teunisson, John N. *Photographic Glimpses of New Orleans.* New Orleans, 1908.

Thwaite, R. G., ed. *Early Western Travels.* 25 vols. Cleveland, Ohio, 1904.

Trollope, Frances M. *Domestic Manners of the Americans.* London, 1832.

Tulane University Architectural School. *Study of the Vieux Carré Waterfront.* New Orleans, 1969.

Twain, Mark [Samuel L. Clemens]. *Life on the Mississippi*. New York, 1874.
Visitors Guide to the World's Industrial and Cotton Centennial Exposition and New Orleans. Louisville, Kentucky, 1884.
Waldo's Illustrated Guide to New Orleans. New Orleans, 1879.
Warner, Charles Dudley. *Studies in the South and West*. New York, 1899.
Wharton, George M. *New Orleans Sketchbook*. Philadelphia, 1852.
Wilson, Edward. *The World's Fair at New Orleans*. Philadelphia, 1885.
Wilson, Samuel, Jr. *Plantation Houses on the Battlefield of New Orleans*. New Orleans, 1965.
———. *Bienville's New Orleans*. New Orleans, 1968.
———. *Vieux Carré Historic District Demonstration Study*. New Orleans, 1968.
Zacharie, James S. *New Orleans Guide*. New Orleans, 1885.
———. *New Orleans Guide*. New Orleans, 1903.

Magazine and Newspaper Articles

Architectural Art and Its Allies (A New Orleans monthly magazine, 1904–1911).
Basso, Hamilton. "Boom Town, Dream Town," *Holiday* 3, no. 2 (1948).
———. "A New Orleans Childhood." *The New Yorker* 30, no. 34 (1954).
Cable, George Washington. "New Orleans," *Century* XXX (May 1885).
Campbell, Edna F. "New Orleans in the Early Days," *Geographical Review* 10 (1920).
Coleman, John P. "Historic New Orleans Homes," a series in the New Orleans *States*, 1923–1925.
Chenault, William W., and Robert C. Reinders. "The Northern-born Community of New Orleans in the 1850s," *Journal of American History*, 51.
Curtis, Nathaniel C. "Early Small Dwellings and Shops of the French Quarter of New Orleans," *American Institute of Architects Journal*, January 1928.
Davis, Rebecca Harding. "Here and There in the South," *Harper's Magazine*, August 1885.
de Rojas, Lauro A. "The Great Fire of 1788 in New Orleans," *Louisiana Historical Quarterly*, 20.
Dunhill, Priscilla. "Expressway Named Destruction," *Architectural Forum*, 126 (March 1967).
Ellis, John H. "Businessmen and Public Health in the Urban South," *Bulletin of History of Medicine*, XLIV, no. 3 (1970).
Kendall, John. "Old New Orleans Houses," *Louisiana Historical Quarterly*, 17.
———. "Sir Walter Scott in New Orleans, 1818–1822," *Louisiana Historical Quarterly*, 21.
Mascot, December 20, 1884; February 28, 1885; and April 25, 1885.
National Trust for Historic Preservation, *Annual Reports* (1967–74), Washington.
"Negro Businessmen of New Orleans," *Fortune*, 40, no. 5 (1949).
New Orleans *Times-Picayune*, July 4, 1976.
Shuey, Mary Willis. "Ironwork of Old New Orleans," *Antiques*, 18 (September 1930).
Sibley, Dr. John. "Journal," *Louisiana Historical Quarterly*, 10.
Treagle, Joseph G., Jr. "Early New Orleans Society: A Reappraisal," *Journal of Southern History*, XVIII.

Unpublished Manuscripts and Theses

Arnaud, Archie W. "Social and Historic Significance of the Names of Streets in New Orleans." Master's thesis, Tulane University, 1936.
Bienvenu, James Robert. "Two Greek Revival Hotels in New Orleans." Master's thesis, Tulane University, 1961.

Bos, Harriet Pierpoint. "Bartholemy Lafon." Master's thesis, Tulane University, 1977.

Caldwell, Joan Garcia. "Italianate Architecture in New Orleans." Master's thesis, Tulane University, 1975.

"Caroline." Letter, 1844. Manuscript, Special Collections Division, Tulane University Library.

Davidson, James D. Diary, 1836. Manuscript, Special Collections Division, Tulane University Library.

Eagleson, Dorothy Rose. "Some Aspects of Social Life of the New Orleans Negro in the 1880s." Master's thesis, Tulane University, 1961.

Everett, Donald E. "Free Persons of Color in New Orleans, 1803–65." Master's thesis, Tulane University, 1952.

Fryer, I. A. Letter, 1833. Manuscript, Special Collections Division, Tulane University Library.

Hardy, Donald Clive. "The World Cotton Centennial Exposition." Master's thesis, Tulane University, 1964.

Kemper, Bishop. Diary. Manuscript. Edited by Julie Koch. Special Collections Division, Tulane University Library, 1932.

Martin, Jerrye Louise. "New Orleans Slavery, 1840–60." Master's thesis, Tulane University, 1972.

Nasitir, Abraham, and James R. Miles. "Commerce and Contraband in New Orleans." Master's thesis, University of Cincinnati, 1968.

Pinnin, Sylvia. "A History of the Irish Channel." Manuscript, Special Collections Division, Tulane University Library, 1954.

Reinders, Robert C. "End of an Era." Ph.D. dissertation, Tulane University, 1964.

———. "A Social History of New Orleans, 1850–1860." Master's thesis, Tulane University, 1957.

Roeder, Robert. "New Orleans Merchants, 1790–1837." Ph.D. dissertation, Harvard University, 1959.

Wharton, Thomas. Diary. Manuscript Collection, New York Public Library.

Index